# Understanding the RSS and the Sangh Parivar

# Understanding the RSS and the Sangh Parivar

Shankar Gopalakrishnan

AAKAR

Understanding the RSS and the Sangh Parivar
*Shankar Gopalakrishnan*



First Published 2018
**Reprinted 2019**

ISBN 978-93-5002-490-4



Published by
**AAKAR BOOKS**
28 E Pocket IV, Mayur Vihar Phase I,
Delhi 110 091
aakarbooks@gmail.com
www.aakarbooks.com

Designed by
Limited Colors, Delhi 110 092

Printed at
Sapra Brothers, Noida

Some parts of this book have been published earlier, including in the books *A Mass Movement Against Democracy: The Threat of the Sangh Parivar* (Aakar Books, 2009) and *Hindutva and Neoliberalism: Fascism, Free Markets and the Transformation of Indian Capitalism* (Aakar Books, 2008).

# Contents

# Introduction

The most powerful political force in Indian politics today is the Sangh Parivar—the family of organisations grouped around the Rashtriya Swayamsevak Sangh. No other Indian political formation has the reach or disciplined cadre base that these organisations have. Whether the BJP wins or loses the next elections, that fact is unlikely to change.

But what are these groups actually fighting for?

There are two diametrically opposed stories one hears about the RSS and its Parivar. The first is that told by its critics. In this view, the RSS is a communal organisation, predominantly aimed at attacking Muslims, Christians and other minorities, and preserving upper caste power within Hinduism. Proponents of this narrative point to obvious facts of history: RSS leaders regularly engage in crudely hate-filled politics against minorities; the RSS has engineered and been closely involved in mass violence; and, from Partition onwards, the Sangh Parivar's role in mass violence in India has been clear and well documented.

But the second story, from its supporters and from the RSS itself, calls the Sangh a voluntary organisation dedicated to patriotism and service. They describe the Sangh as the "largest social service organisation in the world." Various "fact sheets" circulating on the Internet point out how the RSS has volunteered in times of natural disaster, engaged in 'selfless service' to help the poor and the needy, and even helped Muslims at times, while encouraging upper caste Hindus to share meals and spaces with Dalits. They refer to the frequent statements by RSS and BJP leaders about how caste should be eradicated and how all religions are welcome in India. They focus on the RSS's leaders simple lives, lived in honesty, as compared to the general corruption that seems to have pervaded every level of Indian society.

Critics dismiss all of this as an eyewash to cover up the RSS's core of hatred, or as merely a means to recruit people into their hate politics. But the RSS does in fact play multiple roles. Some Sangh Parivar leaders call for violence and killings, while others speak the language of tolerance and coexistence, and some even condemn the calls for violence. Some of its leaders hobnob with corporates and big capitalists, while others lead protests against them. Some call for shared meals, while others endorse upper caste bigotry. Positions and stands are constantly changing.

More importantly, whatever the critics might say, millions of people believe in part or all of the Sangh Parivar's politics. Millions more are sympathetic to it. Finally, millions see nothing particularly wrong with it. The RSS's bundle of contradictory stands has managed to win over huge numbers of people.

The RSS poses a fundamental question to anyone concerned with Indian politics today: why and how has it succeeded in generating this support? Far too much of the time, critics end up answering this question by effectively claiming that all RSS supporters are Hindu chauvinists or dupes fooled by propaganda. This way of answering may be satisfying, but it is not useful—and it is particularly not useful to those who wish to oppose the Sangh.

In this book I will argue that *both* the above narratives are true, or, more accurately, neither is fully true. The RSS is no social service organisation that aims to "serve the country" and help all Indians. But it is also not just an engine of riots and killings.

Rather, it is important to look at two facets of the Sangh phenomenon. First, what the RSS is *actually trying to do*—in its *own* words, by comparison to historical precedents, and as revealed by its organisational methods and tactics. Second, how this political project fits into contemporary Indian history, and where it is likely to go in this context.

When one looks at the RSS from these angles, what emerges is that the RSS is aiming to build *a new consciousness and a new identity* in India—to not merely "unite" Hindus but to *reinvent* them. The RSS is by no means a "backward looking" or "medieval" organisation. It is attempting nothing less than a revolutionary transformation of Indian society. The reason it has become so powerful is not because India needs that revolution, but because other powerful forces in society, for their own reasons, have decided to endorse that vision.

But once we understand that revolution, it also becomes apparent that both the RSS and those who support it are going to fail. The danger here is not that the RSS will succeed in building the Hindu rashtra of its dreams. As we will see here, that kind of society is not only oppressive and brutal; it is, in the long run, impossible. The danger lies in the harm the Sangh Parivar will inflict in its efforts to establish that impossible dream.

The remainder of this book is divided into the following parts. Chapter 1 tries to understand the ideology of the Sangh Parivar from its own statements and texts. Chapter 2 provides a brief history of the origins of the RSS and the other groups in the Sangh Parivar, up to the 1980s (when they became truly national political forces). Chapter 3 places the Sangh Parivar in the broader political context and tries to understand why, in the 1980s, powerful sections of Indian society began to sharply increase their support for the Sangh Parivar. Chapter 4 explores the mass support of the Sangh and its political appeal. Chapter 5 discusses the implications of the RSS's organising methods, and of its politics, for other actors in Indian politics. Chapter 6 discusses the current political situation in India in light of the victory of the BJP in the 2014 general elections. Chapter 7 briefly explores what the rise of the RSS may mean for Indian politics in the near future.

Finally, it might also be useful to clarify what this book is not. Firstly, it is not a handbook to countering the myths and propaganda that the Sangh Parivar spreads. If you find yourself wondering about whether minorities—and particularly Muslims—are indeed as bad as they are portrayed (or if you are looking for responses to these portrayals), you may find the Appendix a useful starting point for the factual situation.

Secondly, this book is also not a comprehensive, detailed history of the Sangh Parivar or an analysis of the structure of Indian politics. On both those points, there are much more detailed and effective books (some of which are listed in the Bibliography).

This book is really only concerned with three linked questions: what does the RSS actually stand for; why is it getting support; and what is it going to mean for Indian democracy?

# 1

# Understanding the Sangh's Ideology

As said above, most analyses of Hindutva begin with the Sangh's propaganda against minorities. However, let us consider a slightly different angle—not what the Sangh affiliates say about minorities, but what they say about themselves.

In 2005, in western Maharashtra, the Sangh Parivar affiliate Vanvasi Kalyan Ashram was distributing training textbooks to young adivasi youth. The aim was to hire them as teachers in the *ekal vidyalayas*, the Sangh Parivar's educational effort in tribal areas (see Chapter 4)[1]. On the back of one of these Marathi language textbooks—titled *Sanskar Varga*—was a kind of oath to be taken by *ekal vidyalaya* teachers:

> We are not working for any specific religion or class but for the entire country. All countrymen are our brothers. All are children of Bharatmata and so long as this feeling is not present in everyone, we will not sit quiet. We will strive to make Bharatmata content and happy. Bharatmata will, like Durga, kill all evil; like Lakshmi, will bring in wealth; like Saraswati, will remove the darkness of superstition and ignorance. Everywhere she will spread the light of knowledge.

---

1. The author obtained these books when affiliated with the Kashtakari Sanghatna, an adivasi mass organisation in Thane district, Maharashtra.

> From the Hindu Mahasagar to the Himalayas, we will spread these seven values throughout the country: unity, hard work, equality, prosperity, knowledge, happiness and peace.

There are many striking things in this passage, but for the moment the most obvious is that there is no mention of Muslims, Christians or "foreigners." It is obvious that the imagery is overwhelmingly Hindu—Durga, Lakshmi, Saraswati, etc.—but for an adivasi youth reading this, there is no reason not to believe the equally strong assertion that the Sangh Parivar is not "working for any specific religion or class."

Similarly, the following quote appears in the now infamous book *Bunch of Thoughts*[2], a collection of writings by M.S. Golwalkar—the second sarsanghchalak of the RSS, commonly known within the Sangh Parivar as "Guruji", and publicly idolised by the present Prime Minister Narendra Modi. When describing "Hindu Rashtra", this is what he has to say:

> As far as the national tradition of this land is concerned, it never considers that with a change in the method of worship, an individual ceases to be the son of the soil and should be treated as an alien. Here, in this land, there can be no objection to God being called by any name whatever. Ingrained in this soil is love and respect for all faiths and religious beliefs. He cannot be a son of this soil at all who is intolerant of other faiths.

Supporters of the Sangh Parivar often quote precisely these kinds of texts as evidence that the organisation is "only" demanding "true secularism." The BJP encapsulates

2. This book was originally published in 1966, but the text used here comes from the third edition, Golwalkar (n.d.). See Bibliography for full reference. It should also be noted that Sangh Parivar supporters occasionally claim that the RSS has 'disowned' this book, but considering that it is available from the RSS website and published by the organisation, that claim appears dubious.

this supposed secularism in its slogan "justice for all, appeasement for none."

Some might describe all this as mere lip service for public consumption. But this is clearly not the case. These quotes, especially the first, come from internal texts used in the Sangh's own training exercises. Indeed, this rhetoric about "harmony" and "unity" is found in practically all the writings of the Sangh's key intellectuals, from its founder R.S. Hedgewar, through Golwalkar and subsequent *sarsanghchalaks*, all the way to Atal Behari Vajpayee and the current *sarsanghchalak* (Mohan Bhagwat).

In fact, as discussed below, if you pick up almost any RSS text—internal or external, public or private—you are far more likely to find this kind of language than you are to find anti-minority rhetoric. It is these concepts that are the core of RSS ideology. Far from being just a "cover-up" of the anti-minority and regressive politics of the organisation, they are in fact at its *root*.

## The Sangh's Notion of "Unity"

In addition to its *sarsanghchalaks*, the RSS venerates a number of other people as leading theoreticians and intellectuals. One among these is Deendayal Upadhyaya, who was an RSS *pracharak* and the former president of the Jana Sangh.

When the BJP was founded, it claimed that Upadhyaya's ideological doctrine of "integral humanism" was its "guiding philosophy" (though these days this philosophy is rarely referred to, notwithstanding the invocation of Upadhyaya as one of India's 'great intellectuals'). Criticising the "West" for adopting "democracy, nationalism and socialism" as its three mutually contradictory principles, he claimed that the 'correct' approach to society would revolve around the following lines[3]:

3. Upadhyaya 1979.

> The first characteristic of Bharatiya culture is that it looks upon life as an integrated whole. It has an integrated view point. To think of parts may be proper for a specialist but it is not useful from the practical standpoint... We do admit that there is diversity and plurality in life but we have always attempted to discover the unity behind them....

Unity in diversity and the expression of unity in various forms has remained the central thought of Bharatiya culture... Conflict is not a sign of culture or nature: rather it is a symptom of their degradation.

From these statements we begin to get a sense of what "unity" and "harmony" for the Sangh Parivar means. This is then amplified by Upadhyaya's subsequent statement in the same lecture:

> In our view society is self-born. Like an individual, society comes into existence in an organic way. People do not produce society. It is not a sort of club, or some joint stock company, or a registered cooperative society. In reality, society is an entity with its own "Self", its own life; it is a sovereign being like an individual; it is an organic entity.

The implications are perhaps clearest when we then find what Upadhyaya has to say about caste:

> Here too, there were castes, but we had never accepted, conflict between one caste and another as the fundamental concept behind it. In our concept of four castes, they are thought of as analogous to the different limbs of Virat-Purusha. It was suggested that from the head of the Virat-Purusha Brahmins were created, Kshatriyas from hands, Vaishyas from his abdomen and Shudras from legs. If we analyse this concept we are faced with the question whether there can arise any conflict among the head, arms. stomach and legs of the same Virat Purusha. If conflict is fundamental, the body cannot be maintained. There cannot be any conflict in the different parts of the same body. On the contrary, "one man" prevails. These limbs are not only complementary to

> one another, but even further, there is individual unity. There is a complete identity of interest identity of belonging.

This analogy between the castes and the body is familiar from many Hindu texts. It is not an accident that Upadhyaya draws on this idea either—caste is central to the definition of both Hinduism and Hindutva (see discussion below). But for Upadhyaya, caste cannot be a source of *either* oppression or conflict. Society is one organic whole, one system in which each individual and each group has a particular function under one overall command. This was perhaps most clearly expressed by Dattopant Thengadi (1979), another Sangh Parivar intellectual, who claimed that "in our system... [social sectors] form an infinite spiral with no inner conflicts and no tensions."

The unity that Golwalkar, Upadhyaya and the RSS are talking about is not, in other words, the "unity" that one normally thinks of when one hears the term. Practically every political organisation invokes "unity"—but normally it is invoked as a *means to an end*. In this normal, day-to-day political rhetoric, we need "unity" for some common goal—"development", cleanliness, progress, struggle against injustice, or whatever.

But for the Sangh, unity is not a means—unity is the *end in itself*. Society is meant to be "unified", it should be "unified", and its failure to be "unified" is the fundamental problem. Inequality, oppression and exploitation are not problems. They are either made up fictions or the results of a lack of unity. In fact there is no injustice in society, and there is no need for social change. What is needed instead is "unity."

The RSS's fondness for equating society with the human body makes a lot of sense in this context. One does not expect one's feet or hands to disagree with one's brain, and if they were to start doing so, that would be a symptom of serious illness. In much the same way, the ideal "unity" that the RSS advocates is the unity of a machine, in which all Indians function "together" under a "brain" without any individual agency of their own.

This vision is then juxtaposed against reality. Real Indian society clearly does not have this "unity"; it is not an "organic entity", it has no accepted "self", and it is divided by countless conflicts, oppression and exploitation. Why is this the case? The Sangh claims that such "disunity" results from two main causes.

The first cause is referred to in the oath of the *ekal vidyalaya* teachers, cited above: superstition, ignorance, confusion, or, as Golwalkar (1979) puts it, a "crisis of character." People have forgotten their history, and been reduced to backwardness and "ignorance". As a result, they have become "selfish", small and petty-minded, and need to be "educated" in "dharma" and brought back to the correct understanding. Without this education they will continue to be disunited and to engage in mutual conflict.

The second cause cited by the Sangh is a familiar one: "outsiders." The Sangh believes that these "outsiders" have taken advantage of the 'crisis of character' in order to spread confusion and disunity. As Golwalkar (n.d.) says, "The utter lack of consciousness among our people of belonging to one country and one culture has made them a fertile field for any scheming foreigner to sow seeds of disruption." The "Bharatiya society" (or the "Hindu nation") has been misled, divided and fooled by these persons.

And who are these outsiders? Golwalkar responds succinctly in *Bunch of Thoughts*: Muslims, Christians, and Communists (more recently, the RSS refers to these as the three "M's"—Muslims, missionaries and 'Macaulayputras'). Muslims and Christians are enemies of the nation because of their "divided loyalties" and their allegiance to invaders.

This logic is the familiar hate propaganda of the Sangh Parivar. It dates back to V.D. Savarkar and the theory that only those who belong to a faith that originates in India—what Sangh supporters today call "Indic" faiths—can be loyal to the country. This is hardly sensible—if it were true, no modern nation except perhaps Israel and Saudi Arabia could exist—but this hate logic does not need, as we shall see, to actually be logical. What matters is the wider purpose that it serves.

In this context, Golwalkar's (n.d.) understanding of "Communism" becomes particularly interesting:

> There are some who feel that the growth of Communism is inevitable so long as economic disparity persists. But the fact is, economic disparity is not the real cause for mutual hatred on which the Communists thrive. The idea of dignity of labour is not properly imbibed by our people. For example, a rikshawala who makes a daily earning of 3 to 4 rupees is addressed as a 'fellow' and a clerk getting but Rs. 60 a month is addressed as 'Babuji'. It is this disparity in outlook in all walks of our life which creates hatred. This is a recent perversion that has entered our life. In our philosophy, there is no distinction of high or low in one's karma, i.e., duty. Every work is the worship of the same Almighty in the form of society. This spirit has to be revived once again.

This notion is striking at multiple levels. First, even as Golwalkar talks of dignity, he simultaneously dismisses any concept of social injustice. The problem here is not that the rickshawallah is earning twelve times less than the clerk, while working harder; but the fact that they are not being addressed with the same language. "Dignity" here is merely a matter of words.

Second, it indicates that the Hindutva approach to social conflict has nothing to do with being "Hindu" as a purely religious identity. Golwalkar is not upset with Communists because they reject Hinduism and religious faith; he makes no reference to that at all. To him Communism is an enemy *simply and only because it "divides" people in its approach,* even though, as he himself admits, there is in fact a difference between a rickshaw puller and a clerk. To him, instead of fighting to change those social injustices, the Sangh should simply impose "unity" and uphold the existing oppression of people (doing otherwise would be against "unity").

While the Hindutva political project is built around a "Hindu identity", what this series of quotes shows us is that hatred for minorities does not simply originate from the fact that they are "against Hindus." At its root, the entire political project of Hindutva cannot and must not accept that there is a possibility of genuine difference and conflict within society.

But there *is* conflict in society, and the only way that can be explained is to draw a line between "society" and the "outsiders" dividing it. *The logic of the politics is such that it cannot exist without an enemy.* The crime of the Muslim or Christian is not to have a different faith, just as the crime of Communists is not that they oppose Hinduism. Hence the RSS's claim that it is "tolerant of all faiths." Rather, the crime of all such persons is that they are the "others" responsible for the "disunity" in Hindu society. Hence the aim of repressing these "Muslims, Christians and Communists" is not to assert Hindu supremacy. It is to unify the "Hindu nation" itself. Slaughtering minorities is a means to the end of a "unified society."

"Outsiders" meanwhile have a clear choice: they can swear allegiance to Hindutva and thus join "society", or they can retain their beliefs, thereby confirming their "foreignness" and making them fit for destruction.

## Social Uplift

Even if the Sangh crushes the "outsiders", though, it still has to deal with the fact that there are oppressed segments—workers, Dalits, adivasis, etc.—within its "Hindu society." How does the Sangh deal with this reality?

The Bharatiya Mazdoor Sangh, the Sangh Parivar's trade union arm, answers this question as follows:

> The national goal cannot be achieved if there exists any feeling of enmity. The BMS. therefore, has deprecated the theory of class conflict and emphasised that all the constituents should act and work in unison. This can be achieved by developing the concept of "family" in the industry.

Once again, the overarching key goal is that there should be no conflict. Instead, society is like a family, where—the Sangh says—the upper castes and capitalist class should function like parents helping their "neglected brethren." The latter term is applied to all sections of the oppressed and the poor, but particularly to adivasis and Dalits, who are seen as backward and lacking in national spirit. Thus, Golwalkar's formula for methods to respond to untouchability is:

> Programmes like bhajans, keertans, festivals, recital of stories from Ramayana and Mahabharata could be arranged, where all Hindus would assemble in a spirit of common brotherhood submerging all such differences as "touchable" and "untouchable" in a current of pure dharmic devotion. Service projects to promote literacy, health, sports, etc., should also be undertaken. Modern techniques like the audio-visual appliances may also be usefully adopted. However, the central point of all these activities should be the appeal to the heart, the emphasis on the unifying and ennobling factors, and ignoring of differences.

As described in Chapter 4, the VHP has followed precisely this formula, and its engagement with caste has been riven with patronising initiatives and internal contradictions. In the world of the Sangh, the solution to any caste or other injustice is "uplift"—charity by the powerful to the "weak", and by the rich to the poor. But above all, the "central point" should be *"ignoring of differences."*

In the Sangh's work among adivasis, this thread emerges very clearly. Every effort is made to deny that there is any difference between adivasi faiths and the Sangh Parivar's version of Hinduism. Adivasi gods are made out to be just different names for mainstream Hindu deities, and their cultural practices said to be the result of "backwardness and ignorance." The Sangh Parivar thus describes their work among adivasis as "giving them back their culture."

Thus the Hindutva approach to social difference and social conflict can be encapsulated in a two faced formula: uplift and "education" for those "inside" society, destruction and elimination for those outside it. Together, these two means are envisaged as resulting in the inhuman "unity" that Hindutva believes is the ideal society.

## The Role of the Sangh

In this vision, what is the role of the Sangh itself? What is its purpose and how should it function? This is how the *ekal vidyalaya* textbook answers that question:

> The aim of the Sangh is to organise the entire Hindu society, and not just to have a Hindu organisation within the ambit of this society. Had it been the latter, then the Sangh too would have added one more number to the already existing thousands of creeds. Though started as an institution, the aim of the Sangh is to expand so extensively that each and every individual and traditional social institutions like family, caste, profession, educational and religious institutions are all to be ultimately engulfed into its system. The goal before the Sangh is to have an organised Hindu society in which

all its constituents and institutions function in harmony and coordination, just as in the body organs.

This is, once again, surprising. In their political texts most political organisations identify their allies and enemies, their goals, and their strategies for achieving the changes they desire. But the Sangh's vision goes well beyond that. As Golwalkar puts it:

> The Sangh therefore has never entertained the idea of building an organisation as a distinct and separate unit within society. Right from its inception the Sangh has clearly marked out as its goal the moulding of the whole of society, and not merely any one part of it, into an organised entity.

The Sangh, in other words, does not aim to *fight* for a "unified" Hindu nation—the Sangh *will become* the "unified" Hindu nation. The Sangh seeks not to change the state and political structures of society but to replace them. All existing institutions are to be absorbed into the Sangh or destroyed by it. It is the Sangh itself that embodies the ideals outlined above—the organic unity of a single body following a single purpose, uplifting its "weaker sections" while destroying its enemies.

This mission statement is the clearest indication that the Sangh is less concerned with defending some pre-existing "Hindu tradition" as it is with producing a totally new one, one in which the term "Hindu" *comes to mean* endorsement of the Sangh's politics. The RSS's own practices—as opposed to its statements—make this very clear. It is a little known fact that display of any Hindu deities is forbidden in RSS shakhas—the only images that are displayed and worshipped are the photos of the first two *sarsanghchalaks* (Hedgewar and Golwalkar), the *bhagwa dhwaj* and a picture of "Bharat Mata" (at the time of writing, for the first time, the RSS website has gone as far as to display the Indian flag as well). Moreover, the RSS's traditional uniform (khaki shorts and a white shirt) is as distant as possible from the traditional Indian dress of any community. It was modelled on the British colonial police uniform. In 2016, at the time of writing, the RSS had finally modified its uniform after ninety years—and it chose to do so by replacing the shorts with pants. There is nothing particularly "Hindu" or "traditional" about either pants or shorts.

But if the RSS is not fighting for the Hindu faith, what is it fighting for? The fundamental contradiction that the RSS confronts is not the existence of minorities and "Communists"—who can, at least in its imagination, be forcibly eliminated. Rather it faces a contradiction with *democracy itself.*

In its ideal form, democracy is not limited to holding regular elections. Elections are means to an end. That end is encapsulated in, for instance, the Preamble to the Constitution of India, which states that "liberty", "equality" and "fraternity" are the goals of the Indian political system. In its ideal vision a democracy is a system where people are free to shape their own individual and collective future through a process of debate, collective action and respect for each other's rights.

But every tenet of this approach is antithetical to the "unity" that the Sangh believes in. For the Sangh, debate and conflict—and therefore individual liberty, which leads to them—are diseases to be eradicated. The Sangh aims to build an authoritarian society, and not merely a society where one dictator rules over everyone; rather, it believes that the ideal society is one where everyone accepts the rule of the Sangh, where the organisation *becomes* society.

## Parallels with Other Countries and Movements

This idea seems both impossible and familiar. It is impossible because conflict, dissent and struggle will always emerge; they are not the product of "outsiders" but of human society itself. But if it also seems familiar, it is because it draws on deep parallels in both Indian and world history.

In India, as noted above, the Sangh's notion of itself is very close to the Brahminical ideal of the role of caste. In this view, caste is a system of assigning each person their "most appropriate" role in society (based, of course, on their 'heritage') and then ensuring that they carry out this task for the "good of the whole." Eighty years ago, in his seminal 1936 book *The Annihilation of Caste*[4], Dr. B.R. Ambedkar referred to this theory as follows:

> It is a pity that Caste even today has its defenders. The defences are many. It is defended on the ground that the Caste System is but another name for division of labour; and if division of labour is a necessary feature of every civilized society, then it is argued that there is nothing wrong in the Caste System. Now the first thing that is to be urged against this view is that the Caste System is not merely a division of labour. It is also a division of labourers. Civilized society undoubtedly needs division of labour. But in no civilized society is division of labour accompanied by this unnatural division of labourers into watertight compartments.... As a form of division of labour, the Caste system suffers from another serious defect. The division of labour brought about by the Caste System is not a division based on choice. Individual sentiment, individual preference, has no place in it. It is based on the dogma of predestination.

Of course, for the Sangh the value of the caste system is precisely that individual preferences have no role in it.

4. This is from an edition published in 2004. See Ambedkar 2004 in the Bibliography.

In this sense the Sangh's ideology draws on very deep-rooted traditions of domination in Indian society.

But the RSS's ideology also sounds very familiar for another reason: this is hardly the first time that such ideas have been attempted in history. The most obvious international parallel, if only because it is the best known, is with the European fascist movements—primarily Nazism in Germany and Fascism in Italy. A similar parallel, however, exists with the right wing Islamist organisations of Pakistan and the Middle Eastern countries. Whether these are actually useful parallels to the RSS is a matter of heated debate. Those who criticise this comparison usually say that all these other groups have killed more people, or are more systematically committed to violence, than the RSS.

But the reason the RSS reminds so many people of the European fascists is not just because it is violent. It is because it shares so many of the same ideas and characteristics. Consider this passage from Mussolini's *The Doctrine of Fascism* (1932):

> The State, as conceived and realized by Fascism, is a spiritual and ethical entity for securing the political, juridical, and economic organization of the nation, an organization which in its origin and growth is a manifestation of the spirit. The State guarantees the internal and external safety of the country, but it also safeguards and transmits the spirit of the people, elaborated down the ages in its language, its customs, its faith. The State is not only the present; it is also the past and above all the future. Transcending the individual's brief spell of life, the State stands for the immanent conscience of the nation. The forms in which it finds expression change, but the need for it remains. The State educates the citizens to civism, makes them aware of their mission, urges them to unity; its justice harmonizes their divergent interests; it transmits to future generations the conquests of the mind in the fields of science, art, law,

human solidarity; it leads men up from primitive tribal life to the highest manifestation of human power.

Replace the word 'State' with 'Sangh', and the resemblance is obvious[5]. The same focus on unity, "harmony", and top down control; the idea of the "nation" as if it is some kind of body, where there is no internal conflict; these ideas are repeated again and again in both philosophies. If one examines the founding texts of organisations like the Muslim Brotherhood, the Jamaat-ud-Dawa in Pakistan, and other such groups, the same patterns appear.

Out of all of these groups, of course, only the Nazis and the Italian fascists ever succeeded in maintaining control of a functioning state for any significant period of time. And in this state they attempted to put into practice precisely these approaches to society and social conflict. Thus, under the Nazis, there was a single trade union for all workers, an association of women, a youth association, etc., and almost all Germans were part of one or the other of these associations. The Nazi party (and the German state, from which it was indistinguishable) coordinated these various organisations. The entire system was organised on lines similar to that of the military, with commanding leaders at each level whose orders were carried out by those under them and eventually by the population. Any political or social group outside these organisations was ruthlessly crushed, especially if it was a workers' organisation or genuine trade union, or if it was formed by the persecuted communities. The Sangh Parivar has attempted precisely

5. Of course, the fact that Mussolini eulogises the state rather than the organisation is itself a major, critical difference between the RSS and the Italian fascists, and a point that many commentators have drawn on to warn that the RSS is not merely an Indian version of European fascism. But the parallel remains.

the same kind of organisational pattern, as discussed in the next chapter.

Beyond organisational patterns, with respect to economic policy and class, the Sangh's founding ideological texts also show strong parallels to the European fascists. For instance, on paper the RSS advocates Deendayal Upadhyay's "integral humanism", which is an almost exact mirror image of the European fascist notion of "organic economics".

Where the present form of the Sangh diverges from the European experience is its approach to economic policies—marked above all by complete confusion—and to the state machinery. Moreover, neither Indian nor world politics offers the same structures or opportunities today that European politics did seventy years ago. In this sense, the lessons of European fascism cannot simply be cut and pasted into the Indian context. Exploring the implications of these ideas and their organisation in India requires us to map how they have shaped and been shaped by India's own history. The next chapter starts this exploration by looking at the RSS's own roots.

# 2

# The Creation and Consolidation of the Sangh Parivar: The Early Years

The Rashtriya Swayamsevak Sangh was founded in 1925 by Dr. K.B. Hedgewar. A member of the Chitpavan Brahmin community and a resident of Nagpur, Hedgewar witnessed a clash between Muslims and Hindus in the city and became convinced that Hindus were "in danger."

Hedgewar founded the RSS in part because of a disagreement between him and the other major Hindutvawadi of the time, V.D. Savarkar, who had coined the term "Hindutva" and founded the Hindu Mahasabha the year before. Hedgewar had been inspired by Savarkar's notion of Hindutva, which held that only those who regarded India as both their "motherland" and their "holy land" could be considered Indians. As seen earlier, this had little to do with the actual religion of Hinduism, and Savarkar had little patience with those who sought to equate Hindutva with Hinduism. His concept, he insisted, was political and about "nationalism", not religion.

Hedgewar believed this was true, and agreed with Savarkar that Hindus had been "weakened" by the divisions of caste, language, differences in faith, etc., and needed to be unified with a new consciousness of Hindutva. He also shared Savarkar's intense hatred of Muslims and the belief that both Muslims and Christians—but especially

Muslims—were "foreigners" and enemies of the Hindu nation. But while the two thus agreed on all the essentials of the concept of Hindutva, they differed on how to respond. Savarkar was more explicitly political and hence founded a political party, the Hindu Mahasabha. Hedgewar, on the other hand, believed that there was first a need to build a "cultural consciousness" of "unity", and that this should be done through careful building of discipline and intellectual leadership. The RSS was to be the instrument for this project.

The RSS held its first meeting on Dussehra in 1925. Only six or seven people attended that initial meeting, at which it was resolved to build an organisation to strengthen the "character" and "defence" of Hindus. Subsequently regular meetings were held in Nagpur, where the RSS created its trademark meeting style of combining physical exercises with speeches and games that propagated its ideology. Some RSS members became *pracharaks* (campaigners) and undertook RSS work and discipline on a full-time basis. RSS members took an oath to serve the *bhagwa dhwaj* (designed after the flag of the Peshwa kings, former Brahmin rulers of the area). At the time, the RSS also began its practice of recruiting adolescent young men and indoctrinating them before they attained adulthood. Strong emphasis was placed on absolute obedience to the leader and to the organisation. Women were—and still are—barred from membership, and full time pracharaks were enjoined to be celibate.[1]

In 1926, RSS members participated in another Hindu-Muslim clash in Nagpur, and over the years that followed the organisation began to grow throughout what is now Maharashtra. In 1931, B.S. Moonje, a politician and Hedgewar's mentor, undertook a trip to fascist Italy and

1. The details in this section are drawn from Jaffrelot 1998 and Basu et al. 1993.

returned deeply impressed by the Fascist youth league's practice of weekly sports and indoctrination meetings, involving youth as young as six. The RSS had already begun moving on similar lines, and it is speculated that Moonje's trip consolidated this approach into what is still the RSS's main form of activity[2].

## The Freedom Struggle and the RSS

By 1939, the RSS had approximately 500 active shakhas and 60,000 members, and had mostly developed the complex leadership structure and hierarchy that it has today. Yet its base remained substantially Maharashtrian and upper caste. In 1939 Hedgewar died and was succeeded as *sarsanghchalak* by M.S. Golwalkar, who—in contrast to his predecessor—was the first to give the RSS a detailed and written ideology.

The RSS's attitude to the freedom struggle offers the first indicator of its later politics. Though Hedgewar was imprisoned in 1921 for his participation in Congress activities, he refrained from such actions after the founding of the RSS, except for participating in the Jangal Satyagraha with the explicit aim of meeting others to draw them into the RSS. In 1930, Hedgewar directed his cadres that they could participate in Gandhi's salt satyagraha in their individual capacity if they wished, but the RSS would not join.

In 1943, the British Home Office said[3] the RSS had kept itself within the "bounds of the law" and "refrained from joining the August 1942 disturbances." Those 'disturbances' were the Quit India movement. At the same time, Savarkar directed his Hindu Mahasabha cadre to stay in their government posts and ignore the boycott calls of the

2. See Casolari 2000.
3. Jaffrelot 1998.

freedom movement. Indeed, just before the start of the Quit India movement, Shyama Prasad Mookerjee, also of the Mahasabha but later the first president of the Jan Sangh, wrote a letter to the British Governor of Bengal saying: "Let me now refer to the situation that may be created in the province as a result of any widespread movement launched by the Congress... Anybody, who during the war [Second World War], plans to stir up mass feelings, resulting in internal disturbances... must be resisted by any government that may function..."

These incidents do not only expose the RSS's false claim to be "nationalist." They also reveal a basic characteristic of the RSS, one of the points on which it differs from its far right Muslim counterparts—the RSS has always been very reluctant to confront state power. Both the Sangh itself and its allied organisations have shown a remarkable tendency to collapse when faced with either state action or a concerted political opposition. In Chapter 4, this is discussed further; this essential timidity reflects the internal character of the Sangh's organising.

Despite staying out of the freedom struggle, the RSS continued to expand its base inside India. During Partition, the RSS played a significant role in fomenting violence and organising the massacres of Muslims in Punjab. Shortly afterwards, the former RSS member Nathuram Godse assassinated Gandhi. As a result, the Sangh was banned for a year. The ban was only lifted after Golwalkar accepted Nehru's condition that the Sangh adopt an internal constitution swearing respect for secularism and abjuring violence.[4] This constitution has hardly been seen since.

Despite its substantial spread in western and northern India, however, at independence the RSS remained very

4. Sangh supporters frequently claim that this ban was lifted due to intervention by the Supreme Court, but this is untrue.

limited in its social base. A 1947 internal Congress report on the RSS stated the following[5]:

> The RSS has been a purely Maharashtrian Brahmin organisation. The non-Brahmin Maharashtrians who constitute the bulk of CP [Central Provinces] and Maharashtra have no sympathy with it... Even in the other provinces the chief organisers and whole-time workers will be found to be inevitably Maharashtrian Brahmins.

Heavily dominated by upper castes, with no mass presence, the RSS was thus essentially a marginal presence in politics even in its home areas.

## The Formation of the Sangh Parivar

Increasingly aware of these limitations, very soon after independence, the Sangh initiated a strategy to break out of these barriers. In keeping with its ideological goal of organising all of "Hindu" society, Sangh cadres were tasked with creating new front organisations for different sectors of society. Sangh *pracharaks* created new organisations for various sectors—the Akhil Bharatiya Vidyarthi Parishad (ABVP) in 1948 for students, the Vanvasi Kalyan Ashram in 1952 for adivasis, the Bharatiya Mazdoor Sangh in 1955 for workers, and so on. This marked the birth of the Sangh Parivar; the number of such affiliated organisations now runs into hundreds.

Of these new front organisations, two were to play a particularly important role. In 1950, Shyama Prasad Mukherjee—a former leader of the now declining Hindu Mahasabha—founded the Bharatiya Jan Sangh. RSS cadres formed a key part of this new party and soon took over its functioning, despite Golwalkar's continuing claims that the RSS was 'apolitical.' The new party drew its mass base

5. Jaffrelot 1998.

primarily from among small traders and industrialists; its politics reflected its base, with calls for greater "Hinduisation", removal of internal economic restrictions, and strict controls on imports.

The other important new front organisation was the VHP, founded in 1964. The VHP was explicitly aimed at becoming the "Catholic Church" of Hinduism, namely a single institution intended to bring together, organise and discipline all varieties of Hinduism and all Hindu religious leaders. The VHP marked the Sangh's first venture into actual Hindu religious practice. The VHP also was the first in a series of institutions—the Vanvasi Kalyan Ashram was another—aimed at imitating what the Sangh perceived as the practice of Christian institutions.

In the wake of the founding of these institutions, the RSS itself retreated from direct involvement in public actions, and today the RSS hardly engages in any public protests or mobilisations of its own. It instead serves as the intellectual nucleus and leadership of the Sangh Parivar system.

Yet, despite the new base brought in by these mass organisations, the Sangh Parivar continued to be socially confined and was limited to some geographical areas. It was not a significant challenge to the Congress or to any other political force in the country, and the Jan Sangh did not succeed in winning elections in any state or in becoming a competitor to the other parties. On a side note, one might note that if the RSS is understood to be representing some kind of basic "Hindu" impulse, this long period of marginalisation also needs to be explained; particularly as it included the aftermath of Partition and two wars with Pakistan, all of which offered ample scope for Hindu chauvinist mobilisation.

The RSS's next breakthrough only occurred with the Emergency in 1975, when the RSS and many of the

Sangh Parivar organisations were banned (along with the Communist Party of India (Marxist), the Jamaat-i-Islami and many other organisations). Once again, during this period, the RSS showed its cowardice in the face of state power by cravenly appealing for the ban on it to be lifted. Balasaheb Deoras, the *sarsanghchalak* of the RSS at the time, wrote to Indira Gandhi congratulating her on the upholding of her election (by a Supreme Court packed with her handpicked judges) and claiming that the RSS had "no connection" with any protests against the Emergency.[6] Today the RSS claims just the opposite.

While the Sangh Parivar was by no means in the forefront of the anti-Emergency mobilisations, it gained a wider base as a result of joining the Janata Party, and the Janata government of 1977–1980 made several Jan Sangh leaders (such as Atal Behari Vajpayee) into Ministers in the central government for the first time. The split in the Janata Party in 1980 was partly a result of the "dual membership" controversy, whereby the other constituents of the party demanded that the Jan Sangh leaders renounce their RSS affiliations. When they refused, the party split, and in 1980 a new party—the BJP—was founded.

Shortly afterwards, the Sangh began a mass expansion that is almost unique in Indian political history. From a still small force, capable of winning only two seats in the 1984 Lok Sabha elections, the Sangh Parivar grew into what was arguably India's largest organised political force by the 1990s. To understand this, we first need a broader framework of analysis.

6. For a description of this by someone who is today one of the Sangh Parivar's foremost advocates—Subramaniam Swamy—see Swamy 2000.

# 3

# The Political Backdrop to the Rise of the Sangh Parivar in the 1980s

As mentioned in the Introduction, most critical analyses of the Sangh focus on the fact that it "divides" people. Opponents of the Sangh that are on the political left are more specific—they say that Hindutva divides the poor and the working classes, making it easier to continue their exploitation. At a certain level, this is certainly true. Anyone familiar with the history of states like Gujarat or Uttar Pradesh, where Sangh-inspired political mobilisations led to violence and killings, is aware of how this violence shattered existing organisations and movements around workers' rights, women's issues and tribal rights.

But this approach still leaves us with some fundamental questions. If the Sangh is such an effective instrument to shatter struggles for social change, why have India's ruling classes not sought to push it from independence? More importantly, if this kind of politics is so transparently against their interests, why do so many poor and working class people themselves support these organisations? And why do so many middle and upper class people do so as well—despite knowing that these groups may one day curtail their own freedoms and rights?

Of course, such questions are hardly unique to understanding the RSS or the Sangh. They are in fact the central questions of all politics—why certain forces emerge at certain times, why they do so despite being apparently opposed to the interests of their own members, and why struggles for social change so often seem to fail.

Far too often, these questions are answered by essentially saying that power is maintained by lies, cheating and deceit, taking advantage of people's ignorance and prejudices. All of this is, at one level, certainly true. In the case of the Sangh, the organisation's consistent use of lies and false propaganda is very well known. But, as discussed in the Introduction, this cannot be the whole answer. Any analysis that presumes that millions of people are either bigots or sheep is a counsel for despair, not a guide to understanding.

In that sense, it is useful to identify what *questions* an effective analysis needs to ask—beyond exposing the lies that the Sangh peddles. Crudely, we can divide those questions into two sets. The first set concerns exploiters and the powerful—which, in the case of a society like India, includes those united by caste, class and gender privilege, and is dominated by India's corporates and big capitalists. In this chapter we explore what the Sangh may have come to mean for these sections. In the next chapter, we explore what the Sangh has meant for its own cadre, and for the millions of those from exploited and oppressed groups (such as workers, Dalits and women) who have come to identify with it.[1] In both cases, the question has to start with history—for the Sangh did not always enjoy the support it does today, either from the poor or from the powerful.

## Classes and Movements in the 1980s

Considering that this book is being written in 2016, many readers might have cause to doubt that last assertion. For

1. The analysis in this section draws heavily on the concepts put forward in the Gramscian theory of hegemony. Please see Gramsci (2014), Jessop (1982) and Poulantzas(1978) for a further discussion of these points.

if there was one thing that was clear in Narendra Modi's election campaign in 2013 and 2014, it was the widespread, extensive and extreme support for the BJP and Modi among India's big business and financial sectors. This is also not anything new. Since the late 1980s, the BJP has consistently drawn its highest share of votes from the richest segments of Indian society and from upper caste men.[2] Even in 2004, when the BJP lost, 42% of the upper middle class voted for it—more than they voted for any other party, and more than any other social segment voted for it.[3] Repeated claims that the BJP is better for business, that Gujarat is the most investment-friendly state in the country, and claims that the BJP will deliver more "growth" have become so familar today that claims of a corporate-BJP alliance are now part of the accepted common sense.

But corporates did not always support the BJP or its ideological predecessors, and certainly did not openly support Hindutva-based politicians the way they support Narendra Modi today. Prior to the 1970s, the Sangh's outfits were regarded as essentially marginal to national politics, and the Jan Sangh was described as the party of small traders. The Congress was indisputably the favourite of India's powerful for decades. While the RSS gained national fame with its role in the post Emergency Janata government, the real shift in the attitudes of large sections of the Indian elite occurred in the 1980s. We start with a brief look at that decade here.

Like most societies in the world, Indian society is not strictly divisible into a class of "capitalists", who control money and property, and a class of "workers" who only survive by the wages they get from working for the capitalists. A large part of Indian society—in

2. Heath, Kumar and Yadav 1999.

3. Yadav 2004.

fact the majority—consists of people who would fall "in between"(though only if one adopts such a mechanical and rigid understanding of class). Most Indians own or access some means of production—such as marginal farmers, small traders, shopkeepers, vendors, etc.—but are either forced to also work as wage labourers or depend, despite their nominal "independence", on larger property owners and businesses for survival. This is why Economic Census data and other government surveys consistently show approximately half, or more than half, of Indians reporting themselves to be "self-employed." Even those who clearly appear to be workers—such as migrant labour or industrial contract workers in the industrial belts—often have land or small homesteads in rural areas that support their families.

In reality, people in this position rarely have much more control over their lives than wage workers, but they also have an interest in preserving the little that they do own. Meanwhile, as a result of their sheer numbers and the slightly greater independence that they enjoy, people from these sections form the core of almost all Indian political formations, forming the centre and politically active mass base of the left, centre and right.

Initially, in the 1950s and early 1960s, the Congress mostly provided an overarching framework for political mobilisation of these sections (and indeed of most sections) in mainland India—that is, excepting the Northeast and Kashmir. Yet as early as the 1967 elections (and much earlier in the southern states), there were already signs that this 'unity' under the Congress was beginning to break up.

By the late 1960s, multiple challenges to Congress dominance began to emerge across the country. These ranged from the Naxalite movements of eastern and central India to the rise of regional parties in the south. As the Congress's own internal organisation weakened under

Indira Gandhi, these and many other movements eventually coalesced into the JP-led movement of 1974–1975 and the huge protests it produced. The Emergency, as with so many authoritarian "solutions" to conflict, only accelerated Congress's decline. With the fall of Indira Gandhi in 1977 and the election of the first non-Congress government at the Centre, the Congress's hegemony in Indian politics was clearly at an end. Even its overwhelming electoral victories in the 1980s could not return it to its position of being *sine qua non* of Indian politics.

What followed the Congress, however, was not and still is not a total takeover by some other single political formation (the rise of the Sangh Parivar notwithstanding). Instead, in the 1980s, India witnessed an explosion of mass mobilisation—"new" social movements, new regional parties, armed uprisings in several major areas of India's periphery (Kashmir, Assam, and Punjab) and eventually the Ayodhya and Mandal mobilisations.

Why did this happen? While the causes varied widely, the largest of the movements in the Indian mainland shared one characteristic: the dominant, or at least leading, presence of "rich peasant" groups. Following independence, by the 1950s, all major states had formally abolished the *zamindari* system created by the British, whereby huge areas of land were handed over to *zamindars* who were both landlords and tax collectors (this system applied in areas under the Permanent Settlement). Though zamindari abolition was far from a complete process, the empowerment of the larger tenants of the zamindars created groups of relatively better off farmers—and this new section was much larger in number than the zamindars and landlords who had, prior to independence, dominated most of rural India. Many of these farmers belonged to the middle castes. This middle caste—peasant bloc went on to become a major force in

Indian politics, a phenomenon first visible in the massive support they provided to the Dravidian movement in Tamil Nadu. In the 1960s and 1970s, these were the farmers who were best poised to take advantage of the Green Revolution, which further stregthened them and solidified their presence in most states in India (except for the Northeast).

But by the early 1980s, these groups faced two primary problems. First, the Green Revolution ran out of momentum and in any case had a very limited reach. Between 1970-71 and 1980-81, productivity in agriculture did not grow at all. At the same time, the number of rich peasant households capable of producing a surplus—that is, producing enough food to cover both their own needs and to generate a profit from sales—was steadily declining. In this decade, the proportion of the national income going to agriculture overall hence fell steeply. With productivity stagnating and revenues declining, this effectively meant that even rich peasants had to work harder and harder just to maintain their existence.[4]

Second, the rise of these communities in rural India was not reflected in a concomitant change in political power. They remained politically under-represented. This was particularly glaring after most states had seen decades of anti-caste movements, led in most cases by middle and middle-upper castes. Despite all this, political power in the Congress continued to be dominated by the upper caste, professional and business classes.

Simultaneously, other sections of the population in a similar position—producing for the market but not large enough to themselves be capitalists—were also being subject to an increasing squeeze on their ability to survive. In general such producers had increasingly become dependent

4. Nadkarni 1987.

on the market for survival, requiring them to also sell either their produce or their labour to survive. But at precisely this time, the government also responded to the demands of big companies (this is discussed further in the section below). The result was rapidly increasing pressure on smaller producers, both in urban and in rural areas.

This combined trend produced a shared interest across large parts of the rural population, which in turn led to the rich peasant-led movements of this period. These movements demanded that the state allocate more resources, subsidies, and other such supports to their forms of production (such as free power, fertiliser subsidies and higher procurement prices for farmers). This was most explicit in the case of the farmers' movements, but it was also—combined with caste and ethnic mobilisation—a critical factor in the rise of regional parties in this period. While such demands mainly benefited the largest producers, they made sense even to the smaller producers, or indeed to any producer who sold any of their produce. The fact that these interests were shared across different levels of producers allowed them to be politically translated as the demands of the community "as a whole"—the linguistic community, the caste community, or the regional community, etc.

These tendencies—and the resulting collapse of the Congress—intersected with the simultaneous rise of movements by a variety of other oppressed groups. Across India, new social movements blossomed among Dalits, adivasis, women, the 'backward' castes, linguistic minorities and others who had been marginalised during the Congress's hegemony. The Congress, led by Hindi-speaking, Hindu upper caste, north Indian leaders, and crippled internally by its autocratic leadership, was driven deeper and deeper into a vicious cycle—unable to respond to any of these new demands, but weakened further by its inability to respond.

As a result, the discourse of "communities" demanding state support became the political common sense of the 1980s. The mobilisations around reservations—first in Gujarat and other states and then at the national level through the Mandal mobilisations—strengthened this discourse. All the new regional parties, such as the Telugu Desam Party in Andhra Pradesh, the Janata Dal factions in various north Indian states and the Shiv Sena in Maharashtra, also spoke this language. We can also see a similar discourse, combined with very different histories, in the rise of armed movements in Punjab and Assam.

## The Response of Capital

At the same time, the large capitalists in India were also changing their positions and politics. Until the 1970s, India's big business owners had built monopolistic large corporations through a close cooperation with the state bureaucracy, relying on state regulation to provide them with guaranteed regional markets for their products. But by the 1970s these companies also began to chafe at the state system, with the continued small size of their markets becoming an obstacle to their growth and to their exports. State regulation also blocked them from easily absorbing smaller companies and producers. The post-1980 Congress regime gradually began to change regulations in order to address these demands. In 1985, for instance, the government promulgated a "New Economic Policy", with tax cuts, lower import duties, export tax breaks and relaxed requirements for permission and licensing of industries.[5]

Thus, at the same time as it came under intense pressure to increase public spending and subsidies in favour of people mobilised in the various 1980s movements, the state also began to withdraw from regulation and taxation

5. See discussion in Chandrasekhar and Ghosh 2000.

of big capital. The combined result was a sharp rise in government spending, together with a 'boom' of consumer consumption (driven by the new availability of goods for the rich) and economic growth. Rural employment grew, agricultural real wages rose, and income poverty decreased; it was an unusual period of "prosperity."

Yet this prosperity was built on a contradiction, for the interests of big business and the interests of the mass mobilisations were fundamentally opposed (though few of the 1980s movements were explicitly anti-capitalist). The demand for greater state support and assistance required state involvement and regulation, as well as allocation of economic resources through political decisions based on favouring "communities." But this was precisely what Indian capitalists, along with the now rapidly rising foreign capitalist presence, were opposed to. They were demanding freedom from all political constraints on their investment, reduction in state spending, the withdrawal of the state from procurement and distribution, and the conversion of India into a unified market.[6] State control over investment and state support for small producers was exactly the opposite of what they wanted.

Throughout the 1980s the Indian state attempted to square this circle, with the result that the state descended deeper and deeper into debt as it both reduced corporate taxes and increased public spending. In 1991, NRIs and foreign financial institutions—the two main sources of finance for covering the increasing negative balance of state funds—pulled the plug by suddenly and rapidly withdrawing their funds. The resulting financial crash became the basis for Manmohan Singh and the then Congress government to begin the process of liberalisation, with the consequences that we know today.

6. Rajagopal 1999 has an interesting discussion of some of the cultural implications of this.

But however powerful big business might be in economic terms, it cannot simply impose its vision on a mass polity, especially one that was increasingly mobilised. The Congress was clearly no longer capable of serving their interests either. A significant and growing fraction of Indian capitalists began to look for a political project that could effectively oppose and contain the "divisive" and collective politics promoted by the 1980s' movements. They found that project in Hindutva.

## Parallels Between the Politics of Big Business and That of the Sangh

On the surface, "free market" ideologies—and similar notions that are usually pushed by those close to large corporates—have nothing in common with the Sangh. "Free marketers" usually talk of individual freedom, economic liberty, global integration and trade liberalisation. The Sangh's stated vision of a united, autocratic society with "swadeshi" (self-reliance) seems very far from that vision.

But these apparent differences hide a deep core of commonality—a core that extends beyond merely the fact that both groups dislike Communists and movements of the oppressed castes / classes. Some of the key commonalities between these approaches include[7]:

- *Reduction of social processes to individual choice:* As discussed in the first chapter, the Sangh reduces social developments to a question of individual choice. Thus the Parivar aims to solve Hindu society's problems by inculcating 'correct values', as exemplified by M.S. Golwalkar's declaration that "there is a 'crisis of character' in our country"; social problems are due to individuals' "demoniac ways", which then give

7. These points are discussed more in Gopalakrishnan 2008.

opportunities to "outsiders" to create "conflict". This is strongly parallel to the "free market" notion that poverty, crime and lack of education are due to "poor choices" made by individuals, induced by "outside" intervention like welfare, trade unions and "populist politics."

- *The state is supposed to exist* ***only*** *as the expression and guarantor of a wider collectivity*: For Hindutva, as we saw in the previous chapter, the ideal state is the guarantor of the Hindu rashtra, a "nation" that exists as an organic and harmonious unity between "Hindus." As Deendayal Upadhyaya[8] once put it, "the state is brought into existence to protect the nation, and to maintain conditions in which the ideals of the nation can be translated into reality." These ideals constitute the nation's "soul", and the "laws that help manifest [this soul] are termed *dharma.*" In turn, a "state cannot be without *dharma* nor can it be indifferent to *dharma,* just as fire cannot be without heat."[9] Replace the term "dharma" with the "market" and once again sees a parallel with the free market approach. The ideal state is the "night watchman", the guarantor of the "market"—the only legitimate collective social activity (every other kind of collective social activity is either "perverse" or "political", with the latter meaning it is illegitimate). The state should express the operation of the market and guarantees it against interference. In fact, it is particularly striking that one finds precisely the same phrase—"night watchman"—as a description of the state by the Sangh intellectual Dattopant Thengadi.[10]

8. Upadhyaya 1979.
9. Upadhyaya 1979b.
10. Thengadi 1979.

- *Divisions within this collectivity are unnecessary and pathological; the only division that is of importance is the line between "society" and its Other, the foreigner:* As we saw in the first chapter, for the Sangh, all divisions "within" society are the work of malignant outsiders or foreigners, aimed at breaking up the unity and harmony of the Hindu nation. In free market theories, as in Hindutva, classes, castes and other identities should never be the basis for any kind of collective action or politics. The fact that they are in fact the basis for politics reflects malign state interference and "political meddling." Welfare agencies, the bureaucracy, the legislature, political parties—all are 'outside' society and responsible for its "pathological" divisions. Political actors are socially illegitimate, and for both Hindutva and the free marketers there is no worse crime than to "politicise" anything.

In short, both these ideologies share one basic feature—their intense, militant opposition to any form of collective social activity other than that controlled by themselves (the Sangh in the one case, and big capitalists in the other). For both, collective politics is the real enemy. In this sense the Hindutva project fit perfectly with what was being advocated by Indian capital during this period—a "unified nation"—with no political mobilisation or politicised differences. Hence the caste, ethnic and regional mobilisations of the 1980s—the real target of both ideologies at this time—came to be portrayed as "divisive", "populist" and against the "national interest."

This increasing support was reflected in the rapidly changing attitude among the urban elite and the English media. The BJP specifically targeted this elite segment and with its claim that the Ayodhya movement was not "communal" but aimed at making India into a "modern" society, a proud, strong nation standing against "sectional"and "vested" interests (meaning, again, the other mobilisations of the time). From the viewpoint of business and finance, this was correct, for it would indeed help to create that what they thought of as the truly "modern" vision: a single, de-collectivised unit with as little state intervention as possible.

This support from urban elites translated into increased support from dominant social sections for the Hindutva mobilisation, reflected in growing endorsement by the English media, financial support, and a rapid increase in the number of "respectable" faces (bureaucrats, military officers, journalists, public intellectuals, etc.) who openly declared their support for it. But in itself this was not enough to convert the Sangh Parivar into a mass political force, though it was a necessary step in that direction. To understand the other half of this development—the growth in the Sangh's mass base—we need to look more closely at the functioning of the Sangh in this period and in subsequent decades.

# 4

# The Sangh's Individualist "Bargain"

In the 1980s, the RSS reinvented some of its old arms and created new ones. Between 1979 and 1981 the Vishwa Hindu Parishad was "relaunched" as a mobilisation platform. In 1980, the BJP was formed after the Janata government fell and the Janata Party disintegrated. The new party, initially vacillated between hardline hate politics and vague notions of "Gandhian socialism", but found its footing by the second half of the 1980s. In 1984, the Bajrang Dal was founded, and it went on to be the most visible and brutal organiser of violence in the 1980s and 1990s.

With these new organisations came a new style of politics. Until the Emergency, the Sangh Parivar had operated primarily on the basis of training and ideological indoctrination, with the RSS remaining the most dominant arm of the Parivar. Now, drawing on its legitimacy and involvement in the JP movement, Sangh Parivar organisations began to stage more protests and public actions. In 1983, the Sangh held large protests against the mass conversion of Dalits to Islam in Meenakshipuram, Tamil Nadu. In the same year the VHP launched "Ekatmata Yatras" from across the country in the name of "national unity." As these protests grew, the Sangh Parivar also began a concerted effort to draw in new recruits and new cadres across the country.

These mobilisations eventually coalesced into the movement for the destruction of the Babri Masjid in Ayodhya. In sheer size, this was one of the largest movements independent India has seen. With lakhs of people on the streets, yatras that drew gigantic crowds, and the capacity to engage in terrible, simultaneous mass violence in cities across north India, the Sangh Parivar had "come of age" as a national force in Indian politics.

But who were these people who came out for the Sangh's protests? While there seem to be very few studies on this issue, it appears from most reports that the Sangh Parivar protests were most popular in urban areas, among the urban lower middle classes and the poor, and in small to medium sized towns. The fringes of urban areas also saw strong participation. However, these actions seem to have met with a weaker response in rural areas (outside perhaps of Uttar Pradesh and Madhya Pradesh). The organised working class in many urban areas were often sympathetic to the movement, but were not its leaders or core base. Geographically the movement was most active in Maharashtra, Gujarat and the Hindi-speaking states. The southern states, Punjab, Kashmir and the Northeast remained almost entirely outside of its ambit

## The New Mass Base

This vague mapping throws up an interesting point: it appears that the Sangh managed to mobilise precisely the social sectors that were not represented by the other movements of the 1980s. However, these people too faced many of the same contradictions and problems that those movements sought to address. Vendors, unorganised sector workers, shopkeepers, small traders, and the like in cities were buffeted by constantly changing prices and at the mercy of big businesses and state economic policies, much as farmers were.

How did the RSS manage to reach these sections, which ought to have had, on the face of it, little sympathy with Hindutva ideology? To those who sought leadership, who sought change, what did the Sangh Parivar groups offer? What could Hindutva say to those facing economic and institutional crises? There is no single answer to these questions, of course, but there is a pattern to the answers that emerge.

The pattern is this, offered here as a hypothesis.

The Sangh Parivar offers people a bargain. Those who join gain real economic and social benefits, involving an increased sense of social importance as well as greater economic and physical security. The RSS and its affiliates offer all the gains that come from being *on the side of the powerful,* doing socially *approved* activities that are also beneficial to their cadre as individuals.

*But,* in exchange, these individuals have to give up all claims to any kind of social or organisational involvement except through the Sangh Parivar. In particular, they have to give up any involvement in struggles *against* the structures that are oppressing them. Their ability to keep all the benefits they have received depends on actually supporting the same structures that have oppressed them, and on being obedient to the leadership. In short, the Sangh will provide concrete, real benefits to those who abandon all identities and all freedoms—except that of being an individual, isolated soldier of the Sangh Parivar.

This doesn't seem either a very unique or a very powerful method of organising. But it contains within it the key seeds of the RSS' Hindutva ideology—and thereby makes people identify their own individual interests with the kind of society that Hindutva wishes to create. The idea is not that everyone in the Sangh carries out this bargain—most don't, as discussed at the end of this chapter—but those that do form a committed core that all other activities are built around.

In the remainder of this chapter, we will look at some examples of this pattern, and then finally ask the key question: why does this work?

## The Ekal Vidyalaya Schools and Sangh Parivar Recruitment Among Adivasis

A good example to start with is adivasis, or "tribals." These are India's poorest and most marginalised communities. For 150 years they have faced consistent dispossession from their homelands and natural resources, driven by colonial forest laws and by takeovers for large projects. Adivasis are estimated to form 40% of those forcibly displaced for large projects in the country. As a result of this history, millions of people live in conditions of utter destitution, driven to starvation, migrating for paltry wages and facing constant casteist and state harassment.

Again, one would not expect people living in such circumstances to see much in Hindutva. For centuries they have been ostracised and discriminated against by mainstream caste Hindu communities; they often have their own distinct faiths. Most of all, they have a history of rebellion and conflict against both non-adivasi communities and the state.

But, after an intense, coordinated and focused effort over the past three decades, the Sangh Parivar has built a massive base in adivasi areas—larger than any other single organisation. If anything clearly shows that the Sangh Parivar is not only about playing on "Hindu sentiments", this fact should be it. Why and how has it succeeded in establishing this base?

The Sangh Parivar's penetration into adivasi areas began, at the national level, in the 1960s (though efforts had begun in pockets much earlier). It initially focused around 'seva' (service) activities such as school building, hostels and medical camps. The Vanvasi Kalyan Ashram trained adivasi youth for 'respectable' professions such as law, medicine or the bureaucracy, ran residential schools and set up its own health centres in adivasi areas. In the early and mid 1980s there was a rapid growth in the scale of these activities, reflecting the increased flow of funds into the Sangh's coffers and the new focus on mass mobilisation. More than eight hundred schools were opened by the VHP in 1983 alone, mostly in tribal areas. The number of full-time activists in the Vanvasi Kalyan Ashram increased by six times between 1978 and 1983.[1]

Such activities offered adivasis a clear avenue to individual advancement and, more importantly, to a sense of being included in "respectable" sections of society. For a community which was otherwise ignored by every mainstream political force and state institution, these are significant gains.

Seeing the success of these activities, in 1989 the RSS formally decided that "seva" activities —primarily targeting adivasis and Dalits—would be among its major methods of expansion. A "seva vibhag" was set up within the Sangh and a senior pracharak deputed to head it.

After the vibhag was formed, it initiated a new activity that is one of the best reflections of how the RSS works in adivasi areas—the *ekal vidyalaya* scheme, which is now a major cadre building activities. *Ekal vidyalayas* are supposedly informal, alternative schools for dropouts from the government schools in adivasi areas, with "one teacher for every school" (hence the name). The "Ekal Vidyalay Foundation"—a US based group set up to fund raise for

1. Jaffrelot 1998

these activities—claims that there are 51,689 *ekal vidyalayas* in operation at the time of writing.[2] The actual number is likely to be far larger.

Many of those who study RSS activities have assumed that *ekal vidyalayas* are just one more example of the "saffron schools" run by the Sangh Parivar's educational arm, Vidya Bharati. But in practice, in many areas the *ekal vidyalayas* do not function very well and it is rarely clear whether children attend continuously. For instance, in 2005, when I was affiliated to the Kashtakari Sanghatna in Thane District, three *ekal vidyalayas* were ostensibly set up at one point but all three ceased to function within weeks. The real importance of these schools is not always the schoolchildren; it is the teachers, or *acharyas,* as they are called.

These acharyas are local educated adivasi youth. They are offered a stable salary in exchange for 'teaching' children, though as said they may not always do that. The work required from those whom we met was very small—evening classes for some children on a few days in a week. For most adivasis, cash income is either earned by migrant labour or, depending on the area, collection and sale of non-timber forest produce. Both of these are difficult and unreliable activities. Hence, even a very small salary is a major attraction in these areas, so long as it is steady.

The training these acharyas receive is not what one might expect. Several of the quotes in Chapter 1 come from the textbooks used in these trainings. Their training is not focused on either education or anti-minority propaganda, but on a "social service" orientation; they are asked to believe that they are working for *gaon vikas* (village development). Simultaneously, however, acharyas are asked to take an oath that they will not join any "political" work and will

---

2. See https://www.ekal.org

not affiliate with any political party. They will only work for the "nation" and for "social unity." "Political" work here was explicitly defined to include not joining any of the other movements and organisations active in the area.

For their acharyas, hence, the *ekal vidyalayas* offer both an economic gain in the form of a steady income, as well as the chance to earn social respect through the performance of 'social service.' Yet, in exchange, they are barred from joining any other organisation in the area. This might seem quite normal in the context of joining a political organisation. But this was supposed to be "seva" work, not politics. Nor was it any kind of a job in any normal sense—the time commitment was small, there was no formal contract, and there was an explicit expectation that the acharyas would also give their time to VHP and VKA activities. These activities were not deemed to be "political" but to be "nationalist."

In short, even before any training in Hindutva ideology, the acharya has already effectively consented to the Sangh's basic principles: the Sangh Parivar groups represent true nationalism; any move to assert an independent politics or an independent identity is to be a traitor to one's own interests, since it means the loss of a salary; and all politics except that of the RSS is anti-national and divisive. The subsequent training in Hindutva ideological beliefs is, therefore, far easier.

In our area this training only began with the third round of training provided to the "teachers." Moreover, in this training and in all Hindutva activities among adivasis, the Sangh Parivar systematically rejects any notion of the distinct history of adivasis, of their indigenous faiths or of their struggles against colonialism and caste oppression. Instead, Sangh Parivar groups describe them as "girijans" or "vanvasis" (literally, forest dwellers, as opposed to the term "adivasi", which means first dweller). They insist that they are 'backward' Hindus who need to be educated in the faith. Such insults to a tradition might normally be expected to meet fierce resistance—and in areas with active adivasi organisations, they do. But where such organisations don't exist, the choice before an adivasi youth can often be between receiving the Sangh's benefits—security, money and access—or defending an intangible history and culture that they may themselves feel alienated from. By identifying the ideology with real gains, belief in the ideology becomes much easier, and the Sangh Parivar does not lie when it says that it has many adivasi leaders.

## Recruitment of Dalits

When it comes to Dalits, the Sangh seems to operate at a superficially different level. When the VHP was expanding in the 1980s, one of its first initiatives was to organise two "Jnana Rathams" in Tamil Nadu (as a response to the mass conversion of Dalits to Islam in the town of Meenakshipuram). These mobile vans carried images of the Tamil deity Murugan—but in each village the VHP insisted that Dalits would wash the idol. In the same period the VHP planned to build 100 temples in Dalit areas.[3] In 1983, the RSS launched a new group known as the "Samajik Samrasta Manch" on April 14th—Ambedkar's birth anniversary. In the Ekatmata Yatras that then preceded the main Ayodhya mobilisation, Dalits were frequently asked to carry the holy water brought from the Ganga.[4] During the subsequent Babri Masjid protests, the Sangh yatras would deliberately traverse Dalit areas in each city.[5]

3. Jaffrelot 1998.
4. Jaffrelot 1998.
5. Lochtefeld 1996.

Similarly, as Golwalkar himself emphasised in the previous chapter, the Sangh has long promoted shared meals with Dalits. It is a common practice for Sangh Parivar leaders to make public events around having shared meals or, more rarely, eating in Dalit households. In 2016, BJP MP and RSS ideologue Tarun Vijay was beaten up after twice leading Dalit groups into temples in Uttarakhand[6]. Similarly, since the 1980s, the Bajrang Dal has focused on recruiting Dalits and describing them as defenders of the Hindu community. In this sense, the public actions of the Narendra Modi government—talking of Dalits as brethren, welfare schemes for Dalits, special shakhas for Dalit areas—are nothing new for the Sangh Parivar.

In sum, all Sangh groups take steps towards *access* for Dalits and other members of oppressed castes to *high caste* or *public* spaces. They also involve symbolic gestures towards respect, such as permitting Dalits to wash idols or enter temples. Such moves are far from being irrelevant or meaningless. For Dalits, untouchability and denial of access to public space are extreme, daily reminders of the lack of respect for their dignity in Indian society. They also have very physical consequences—including violence—and economic ones, by denying access to state facilities, water supplies, cremation grounds and other daily necessities.

On the surface, then, these appear to be genuine confrontations with casteism. But in reality, they address one basic contradiction of caste while denying all the others. Caste is not only about access to space and respect. It is an *economic* system built around segmentation and control of the workers and producers of society—as Dr. Ambedkar observed in 1936 (see quote in Chapter 2). But the Sangh, once again, tries to reduce caste to an *individual*

6. See *Hindustan Times*, May 20, 2016.

question—do as we say and we'll treat you with respect. But we won't address any of the foundations of caste, and we will not permit you to do so either.

But in the case of caste, this blossoms into a major contradiction. The total marginalisation of adivasis from the political and economic system—and most importantly their consequent lack of defined position in the caste hierarchy—allows the RSS to simply invent new categories and terms for them ("girijan", "vanavasi", etc.) But for Dalits and other oppressed castes, the opposite is true—their position in the caste system, and therefore in the social division of labour, is very clear indeed. Since the Sangh Parivar's notion of social organisation requires the reproduction and continuation of this division of labour, these communities must therefore continue to fulfil the degrading and oppressive social roles assigned to them—even as the Sangh talks of brotherhood at the same time. This leads to egregious absurdities such as Narendra Modi's statement about the Valmikis, a Dalit caste whose traditional occupation is the collection of nightsoil[7]:

> At some point of time, somebody must have got the enlightenment that it is their [Valmikis'] duty to work for the happiness of the entire society and the Gods; that they have to do this job bestowed upon them by Gods; and that this job of cleaning up should continue as an internal spiritual activity for centuries. This should have continued generation after generation. It is impossible to believe that their ancestors did not have the choice of adopting any other work or business."

More importantly, it also leads to direct political clashes—as in the post 2014 beatings of Dalits skinning cows by *gau rakshak* groups (discussed in further detail in Chapter 6). This violence exposes the contradiction at the heart of the Sangh strategy. The Dalits in question are, of

7. Quote taken from Shah 2007.

course, engaged precisely in their prescribed occupation. But this occupation contradicts the Sangh's "Hindu identity" symbology—namely, the cow—which is being used to provide extortion money, power and status to unemployed youth through the *gau rakshak* campaign.

Hindutva ideology has no answer to this paradox except to return to talking of 'uplift' and 'brotherhood'. That is, it tries to lure *individual* Dalits with the promise of specific gains, while simultaneously upholding the caste system as such.

## Targeting Urban Women

Urban women, especially those of middle caste and lower middle class sections, have also been specifically targeted by Sangh Parivar organising. In large parts of India, women from these caste and class backgrounds are strongly discouraged from entering public spaces and public activities—leave alone participating in politics. In the author's own experience of lower middle class households in north Indian cities, women are often forbidden to even open the door.

The Sangh Parivar has specifically targeted such women, both through their general public actions and through the "women's wings" of the VHP and the RSS (the Durga Vahini and the Rashtriya Sevika Samiti respectively). These groups specifically reject any notion that they are "feminist" organisations or women's groups. Rather, they present themselves as "respectable" organisations engaged in—once again—social service, training and assistance to help women and "defend their honour."

This approach makes these groups more appealing to the *male* members of the family, giving the sense that involvement with them offers a "safe" avenue of political action for women. Women are hence able to join such work, often starting with 'service' roles, without facing family opposition. Several factors play into such an appeal—the fact that the women's wings are clearly subordinate to and therefore 'protected' by the Sangh Parivar's male organisations; the linkages to religious festivals and public gatherings, which are traditionally one of the few spaces that women can be involved in; and, perhaps most importantly, the fact that these groups explicitly eschew any challenge to patriarchy, family relations, and violence against women.

Even as women are mobilised in public by Sangh organisations, they will often do so by *reprising* traditional gender roles *in the public activity itself.* Thus, during the Ayodhya mobilisation, women were organised to "send off" male *kar sevaks* with special ceremonies consisting of garlands, specially prepared food, and prayers for their survival—echoing what women would supposedly do for departing armies in Hindu mythology.[8] The Sangh Parivar also appears to offer leadership roles to women, but many of those who attained that position—and particularly those who did so in the 1980s—were sadhvis who had specifically "renounced" their roles as family providers and hence were permitted to be publicly active. Sadhvi Rithambara, Uma Bharati, Sadhvi Saraswati, and more recently Sadhvi Prachi are among the best known examples.

In this sense, with women one sees both the strategies used with adivasis and those with Dalits at work. The emphasis on "social service" provides a safe but simultaneously empowering space—within the confines of the existing order. And, just as in the case of Dalits, this empowerment comes to *individual women* while simultaneously trying to *reinforce* the oppression of women in general.

8. Basu 1998.

Thus, the Sangh Parivar's rhetoric around women always focuses on their role as mothers—with both male and female VHP and BJP leaders declaring repeatedly, since 2014, that Hindu women need to increase their birth rate to "keep up with the Muslims." Sexual violence against women is interpreted as a problem either of their "character" or as a result of the failure of men to protect them. Anything that challenges the oppression of women as such—for instance, the BBC documentary *India's Daughter*, on the 2012 Delhi rape case—is attacked for "showing the nation in a poor light" or being "divisive." It is not an accident that the only time the BJP has used unambiguous rhetoric around women's rights is in its attack on the practice of triple *talaq*—among Muslims.

The overall message is clear, as it is among adivasis and Dalits: in exchange for abandoning collective identities and political struggle, one will receive certain limited social and material gains, gains that can be crucial to survival. Yet those gains will remain forever precarious, for they are dependent on staying with the Sangh Parivar, not questioning social power relations, and obeying the increasing demands of one's organisation. Disloyalty or dissent means not just expulsion, but loss of all that has been gained.

## Why Does This Work?

It is easy to dismiss those attracted by this as being too short-sighted or too ignorant to understand what they are getting into. But this overlooks the more powerful appeal that the Sangh Parivar offers. The examples discussed above illustrate two factors that apply across many class, caste and gender configurations in India—and that make this half-empowerment seem more attractive.

The first factor is the fundamental *insecurity* in which the majority of Indians live their lives. Those in daily wage and casual labour suffer this in the most extreme fashion, where income literally varies from day to day and every bit of income has to be chased for security. Then, the petty commodity producers discussed in the previous chapter each face their own forms of insecurity—some natural, such as rainfall and seasonal variation for small farmers and those dependent on them; and some human, such as police extortion and harassment in the case of traders in the city, or fluctuations in customer demand.

This is not just a question of economics. Insecurity becomes a form of *indignity*, as your security and that of your family comes to depend on other people—those who buy from and sell things to you, those who protect you from mafias, those who provide you with public services like ration cards and electricity connections, and so on. The result is a constant sense of being a lesser human being. This reality is related to poverty, but it is not limited to it. Only a minority of Indians live lives without facing it. The "reforms" after 1991 have also had the effect of increasing this insecurity in multiple ways. Over the past two decades, there has been almost no growth of permanent and secure jobs in India. Government recruitment—the most secure form of employment for most in India—has also slowed and in many departments has completely stopped. Agricultural and food prices have become much more volatile as a result of the opening of India's markets to trade. Public investment in public services, agencies, and credit has also dropped sharply, especially in rural areas. All this has led to the present-day agrarian crisis, marked in the most terrible manner by the prevalence of farmers' suicides.

How one responds to this situation of insecurity is varied; it depends both on each individual's history and choices, and on the opportunities available in their political environment. The most common response is the dependence on political and local leaders, who become patrons, dispensing assistance and security to their supporters. When in trouble with the police, in need of some basic facility, or when being threatened by a state agency, people turn to politicians for help. In urban India—with its relatively higher levels of immediate insecurity, violence, and lack of social support networks—such patronage is a basic requirement for survival for a large proportion of the residents. In passing, one should also note that this is one of the crucial divisions in Indian public discourse; an English-speaking urban professional may not even know the name of their municipal councillor, but that would be inconceivable for most urban Indians.

This is also the default mode of organising for most Indian political parties. Ideology is not irrelevant or meaningless—it dictates the way that the leadership operates, the social classes it operates with, and so on—but the nitty gritty of daily work consists of political leaders engaging in direct *quid pro quos* with their political base, "getting things done" in exchange for public support and votes.

A second form of response is collective organising—whether through formal groups like trade unions, social movements or parties, or in smaller collectivities and associations. Caste networks are one, often invisible, but critical form of such organising. These groups provide mutual solidarity and assistance, along with varying degrees of a larger political vision. During periods of widespread struggle, such as during the 1980s movements discussed in the previous chapter, these groups can become major sources of security for those involved. But the problem is that any effort by these groups to generate genuine social change involves confronting power in one form or the other, and that can mean greater insecurity and greater sacrifices—all for the uncertain promise of an eventual victory. Where such mobilisations fail, the sense of disillusionment and indignity that follows can be greatly magnified as well.

The Sangh model of organising has a distinctive form of appeal in this context of overall insecurity. It essentially follows the same model of individual patronage that every political leader follows—but with a crucial difference. Here the patronage is not by one or the other leader, but by the "good" people, the socially *superior* castes and individuals. Hence the Sangh's constant emphasis on 'character' and 'decency', which are defined in exclusively Brahminical and male terms. Membership in the Sangh means access to social circles that were never accessible before—as we saw in the case of women and Dalits—and access to positions of leadership and power that were not accessible either. Along with this access comes economic and social benefits, such as salaries to the *ekal vidyalaya* teachers and bribes to *gau rakshak* extortionists (not to mention the opportunity to loot during violence). The resulting power can be extremely useful in the face of daily insecurity. The Sangh thus offers both the advantages of patronage and that of having a larger, organised force with you, and more importantly it does so in a manner that is approved by those who are socially powerful—including, most importantly, the state machinery.

In sum, the Sangh's bargain is to offer its cadre the chance to be someone they never thought they could be—*but only if they give up any chance of challenging the structure that prevented them from being so in the first place.* Hindutva ideology reflects this dilemma (and creates it) by declaring that injustice does not exist, it is only the product of ignorance on the one hand and evil outsiders on the other. So real social justice also does not need to exist. All one needs for a life of security is to obey the Sangh, for which one will be rewarded. The Hindutva ideology and the RSS identity becomes a code word for this kind of half-baked empowerment, one that is real and significant, but which is also endlessly precarious.

## The Sangh Parivar and Mass Politics

It might be objected that the Sangh Parivar cannot directly approach every one of the tens of millions of people who support them and make such offers. Nor are all of their supporters drawn in by such calculations. Indeed, one might argue that the majority are not.

But mass politics of any kind—left or right—is not about making the same offer to every one of your supporters. Rather, successful political formations operate by building a *core* of committed, strong supporters and then using that core to reach out to wider and wider audiences. Every successful political party consists of several concentric rings of leadership and activity.

In the Sangh Parivar, this core is constituted through the above bargain. Around this core, the BJP then brings in another huge mass base through the normal operations of any political party—patronage and protection for supporters, enabling corruption, competing in elections, campaiging in the media, etc. The ABVP does the same, operating as a 'normal' student organisation that takes up local student issues as well. Each of the other Sangh outfits hence adds to the overall base. But since the leadership of all these organisations is constituted by people locked into the basic Sangh Parivar organisational pattern—and in most cases are locked into the RSS itself—the overall structure operates in a remarkably effective manner, with all the other groups acting as ideological transmission belts for the committed core cadre.

The result is the sheer size of the Sangh Parivar, and, today, its seemingly omnipresence and invincibility. Anyone who does not like the saffron agenda today finds themselves feeling like a small minority, outshouted and outgunned by what seems like a gigantic force that has penetrated every part of the country and every part of public life.

But all this fire and brimstone obscures the fact that that central core can't grow—or even survive—without one central precondition. That precondition is the support of the three primary institutions of social power—capital, the state machinery and the institutions of public opinion (most of all, the media).

The support of capital, as we saw, is necessary at two levels. The first is practical; Sangh-style politics requires, contrary to their images of austerity, significant amounts of money. Festivals, "social service", school networks, public rallies, salaries, patronage, and so on all require access to funds. This is one reason that the Sangh has extensive international networks that fundraise in other countries as well, usually in the name of "social service" and "development work".[9] Internally, donations from traders, companies and the locally wealthy are integral to Sangh organising in most areas.

But far more important than this fundraising role is the second role that capital plays. The implicit support of big business influences both the position of the state and of mass media. This in turn is even more crucial to RSS' style organising.

For the most basic requirement for any kind of Sangh Parivar politics to succeed on a large scale is that *the state*

9. Two such affiliates are the India Development and Relief Fund in the US and Sewa International in the UK, which both claim to be funding 'social work', development initiatives and alternative education in India; while in fact almost exclusively supporting Sangh organisations.

*should not systematically act against it.* The entire bargain that the Sangh Parivar offers falls apart if joining it means risking arrest or harassment. The cadre base is built on individuals seeking the sense of security and benefits that it provides; if that security and benefits begin to diminish, it risks disintegration.

This is why, if one notes carefully, the Sangh Parivar very rarely attempts to directly confront state power. Whenever any state institution initiates an actual effort to stop them, these groups flee the scene with astonishing speed. We have already seen how RSS leaders pleaded with the central government to lift the bans on it. Every Sangh-created "riot" and mass killing ends as soon as the police decide to actually act. This is also why states like Bihar and West Bengal—where, for various reasons, ruling parties decided not to allow Sangh mobilisations in the 1990s—suddenly witnessed "communal peace" in that decade after brutal mass killings earlier. Despite grave threats about thousands giving their lives for a Ram temple in Ayodhya, since 1992 neither the VHP nor any other Sangh Parivar outfit has ever taken any action for that temple that would involve confronting the state.

Similarly, in areas where strong popular movements or other political parties confront them, their expansion is greatly limited. In Kerala, despite constant effort for decades, the BJP has only now managed to win a single MLA seat—and that too only at a time when it can pitch the central government's open support for it, against the opposition of the Left parties in the state. Where the Sangh Parivar cannot claim to have state approval, it finds it very difficult to expand at all.

Finally, there is the mainstream and mass media, which the Sangh once again requires to maintain its air of "honesty" and "decency"—or, more accurately, approval from the general political discourse. The Indian media is in any case dominated by upper caste Hindu men. In the 1980s, as capital swung into support for Hindutva, the media swung with it. The Sangh also mounted a systematic attempt to ensure that Sangh sympathisers entered media outlets, particularly in Hindi and English, and in the burgeoning TV media in the 1990s. Takeover of television spaces was a part of this effort, and one study has in fact identified Doordarshan's serialisation of the Ramayana in 1989 as a key facilitator of the rise of the Ayodhya movement.[10] The combined impact of the shift in the position of capital and the urban elite with this strategy has meant that there are hardly any media outlets in India today that are willing to portray the Sangh with any degree of objectivity. Its every act of killing is described, at worst, as 'extremism' or "communal violence." Thus we have a political discourse today where the mass murder of thousands in Gujarat or Bhagalpur is a 'riot', while even peaceful protests by Kashmiris are described as "terrorist" acts.

As discussed in the previous chapter, the political situation of the 1980s made the support of capital and the media available, and the Sangh then exploded into political prominence, manipulating and building upon these favourable circumstances. Today Hindutva tropes have so totally infected Indian public discourse today that the Sangh has essentially achieved exceptional status—the sense that it can get away with anything, since it is the repository of the "national good."

But this also shows how fundamentally *brittle* the Sangh Parivar actually is. It can only offer anything up to the point where there is no genuine alternative. It cannot confront state opposition. It struggles to handle significant political

---

10. Rajagopal 1998.

opposition. It flees as soon as it is systematically confronted by anyone. Underneath its giant size lies a paper tiger.

This is not a surprise. Adherents of ideologies like these have always had this characteristic. After the end of the Second World War, when the leaders of the Nazi party were put on trial at Nuremberg, only one chose to defend the Nazi ideology: Julius Streicher, who was a cartoonist, not a party leader. The real leaders spent the trial denouncing each other and competing to claim that they had tried to mitigate the worst effects of the Nazi regime. Asked to explain the regime which had destroyed Europe and large parts of the world, the government which once claimed it would rule for 1,000 years, these leaders had nothing to offer but venal self-justification. The flip side to this form of politics is always cowardice.

In the remainder of this book, we explore what this brittleness means for the RSS and for India today.

# 5

# Implications of an Impossible Dream

Given all that has been discussed in the previous chapters, the Sangh Parivar's expansion has led to far more than just creating an atmosphere of communal tension. In this chapter we explore some of these implications in greater depth. Most of them flow from the basic contradiction at the heart of the Sangh project: how do you create your dream world if that dream world is impossible, and what does it mean for everyone else when you try to do so?

## Implications for Other Kinds of Politics

As discussed in Chapter 2, the logic of the Sangh's politics requires that there always has to be an external enemy, an 'outsider' who is responsible for *both* injustice and conflict. This is the key difference between all the Sangh's "social service" activities and those of a genuine 'service' organisation—the latter does not need to mobilise either its cadre or its beneficiaries in "defence" of anything or "against" anyone. But the Sangh always has to do so. Hence even schools or healthcare centres will be accompanied by quiet discussions on Sangh ideology and the need for "unity" in the face of the "outsider."

This produces implications for local politics. The Sangh needs to have someone to mobilise against. This mobilisation doesn't always have to be public—it can simply be something that the Sangh keeps planning. But it needs to exist, or the ideology becomes difficult to propagate.

Such mobilisation becomes especially important to the Sangh Parivar when the target is another social organisation that presents an alternative or liberatory ideology. The targeting of such groups then becomes doubly imperative as any prospect of genuine empowerment, or genuine struggles for justice, greatly weakens the Sangh's appeal. Delegitimising these groups is hence vital.

A small example from the author's own experience might help demonstrate this. In the town of Chamiyala, in Tehri Garhwal district of Uttarakhand, a people's organisation called Chetna Andolan[1] has been running a school called the "Jagdish Joshi Dream School for Child Education" for over a decade. The RSS has also been running a Saraswati Shishu Mandir near the town for several decades.

Periodically, Sangh organisations have alleged that the Dream School is a missionary initiative and that it is entirely aimed at "corrupting" local children and "converting" them to Christianity. This allegation is simple fiction—the school has no link to Christianity, missionaries or any religious institution, and does not receive any foreign funds. But the RSS and the SSM staff would return to this point every few years. Most recently, in 2016, following the Andolan's successes in various mobilisations in Uttarakhand, the RSS became even more active on this front. It took out a small march of costumed protesters in Chamiyala town calling for all "foreign" and "anti-Indian" education to be banned. SSM staff also personally visited the households of most of the parents of children in the Dream School, hinting to them that there were secret and dangerous dealings at the

1. The author is affiliated to the Andolan.

school, and it would be better if they sent their children elsewhere. Forty-two families did eventually withdraw their children, though ironically none were sent to the RSS school as a result (they were sent to other schools in the area).

This is a minor, small-scale example of the kind of activities that Sangh affiliates engage in on a regular basis. Every area with a Sangh presence sees such campaigns frequently, with the usual targets being minority religious and educational institutions and other social movements. With the rise of the BJP government in 2014, this is now being translated to national politics—Sangh affiliates are constantly hurling allegations like "anti-national", "seditious", "terrorist", "Pakistan sympathiser", "Naxalite" and so on against a range of targets. The implications of this kind of national fear mongering are discussed in more detail in the next chapter.

The real target of the Sangh's allegation hurling here is not just the target group. The far more dangerous implication by the constant repetition of such propaganda—and, more importantly, the utter lack of response to it from the government—is the implication that the government is either incapable of stopping malicious activity or is conniving with it. Coupled with the Sangh's own offer of 'security' and status to its cadre, this adds up to a basic message to the Hindu population of the area that if they want to survive, they have to buy into the Sangh's half-baked empowerment offer. Doing anything else means either falling prey to nefarious designs or, even worse, becoming an enemy of the Sangh Parivar yourself. For local and regional politics, this generates an atmosphere of fear, suspicion and simmering violence.

Ironically, all of this is only possible where the state machinery itself connives with this kind of behaviour. This reflects the shifts discussed in the previous chapter.

The police are the most dangerous in this regard. In both BJP-ruled and non-BJP states (though naturally far more in the former), the police will facilitate RSS campaigns by registering cases and supporting fear mongering against targets. Perhaps most importantly, they will almost always refuse to act against Sangh Parivar groups engaging in intimidation and violence.

These tendencies together have two simultaneous effects. The first is to delegitimise and obstruct not only minority institutions, but any kind of alternative politics and struggles for social change. It undercuts the common social institutions that make mutual trust and dialogue possible—which all rely on the state, at the end of the day, to be the guarantor of security. In an atmosphere of mutual suspicion and imminent violence, with the police acting in a partisan manner, popular organising—in any case a difficult task—becomes much more difficult. The RSS's attempts to replace the state as the ultimate arbiter of safety undermine the foundation of democratic politics as a whole.

The second is to reinforce the sense of the Sangh Parivar's status as the most powerful organisation in society. The Sangh seeks to create a situation where only activities it permits are regarded both as legitimate and, more importantly, as *feasible*. Decades of this kind of organising culminates in the mass violence of riots and pogroms, when the Sangh Parivar's claim becomes literally true: anyone who actually stands up against Sangh affiliates can simply be killed.

This dismal picture is only one side of the equation, though. The other side is that such strategies cannot continue forever. In the name of establishing security, the Sangh's tactics actually create a new form of *insecurity*—in the form of continuous tension, instability and violence. It ends up in a race to try to prove that its offer of security is worth the cost it inflicts. That can only be true as long as state connivance is total and opposition is weak or non-existent; and there is no way to guarantee that the latter, in particular, will always be true.

## Implications For "Hindu Identity"

Given all the factors discussed in the preceding chapters, the Sangh's relationship with the actual practice of Hindu religion is complex and often contradictory. The Sangh Parivar's project of a "unified" society that offers most of its members "conditional" security—conditional, that is, on obedience to itself—has no roots in the religious *practice* of Hinduism as such, beyond the caste system. Hence symbols for it have to be essentially invented, without straying too far from existing traditions. In this, the Sangh has had tremendous success—once again, as noted, because of the complicity of the state machinery and the media.

The inherent contradiction that the Sangh faces in this process is that, of course, established Hindu symbols and ceremonies do not equate to symbols of membership in the Sangh. Hence the Sangh almost always tries to choose symbols that are recognisably "Hindu" but are not directly worshipped by many people. The cow and "Bharatmata" are examples.[2] They also introduce new practices, such as *shuddhikaran* for "reconverting" people from other religions to Hinduism—a practice borrowed from pre-independence Hindu social reform movements. Even the figure of Rama was specifically reportrayed by the Ayodhya mobilisation.[3]

In addition to promoting new symbols, the Sangh Parivar also pushes a picture of the Hindu faith that

2. Lochtefeld 1996.

3. Davis 2005.

is intended to relate it to the question of identity—and hence the importance that the Sangh Parivar attaches to the question of religious conversions. The idea that the Hindu faith does not convert, and is hence under threat from "aggressive" and "Abrahamic" religions that do, dates back to the colonial period and was a major theme of the Hindu reform movements of the time. But in independent India, there has been no significant change in the proportions of various religious communities that is not related to demographic factors (such as increased poverty and discrimination resulting in slightly higher growth rates among Muslims—which, notably, are not as high as the growth rates among adivasis, for instance, who face even more poverty and discrimination). Aside from the basic question of how conversion can be seen as a problem if one believes in freedom of belief, there is simply no evidence of a vast organised conspiracy that might threaten the Hindu faith in any sense. But the Sangh Parivar has managed to make this non-existent "problem" into such a significant political issue that, in 2004, 56% of Hindus agreed that "there should be a complete ban on religious conversions".[4] Today, the "does not convert" notion has become a central part of the self-definition of many Hindus. The ultimate irony is that the largest public conversion activities in the country today are implemented by the Sangh Parivar itself, in the name of its so-called "ghar wapsi" activities.

It is a truism that every aggressive right wing ideology manages to make majorities feel like minorities and the powerful feel like they are victims. This kind of political generation of religious identity is not unique to the Sangh—it is typical of every "fundamentalist" political formation anywhere in the world. But it once again reinforces the

4. Palshikar 2004.

fact that the Sangh does not draw on Hindu identity as much as it *invents* it. In this sense, calling the Sangh a "Hindu supremacist" or "Hindu nationalist" organisation is misleading. The new "Hindu" being invented by the Sangh would not have been recognisable as Hindu at all a century or two ago.

## Implications for Capital and the Financial Sector

In Chapter 3, we saw the potential the Sangh's form of organising had for breaking the vocabulary of communities, subsidies, state support and collective action that had posed a potential risk for the expansion of big capital in the 1980s. Many commentators implicitly assume that the battle was won in 1991. That year saw the onset of "economic reforms" and the gradual withdrawal of the state machinery from licensing, price regulation, public investment, and so on.

But the transition in 1991—massive as it was—was far from total. Indeed, at the *political* level, that change has not been completed to this day. Even today, India has no party that unequivocally defends the policies being advocated by big business and finance. Commentators who support "economic reforms" often lament that India has no "Margaret Thatcher" (aside from those who, without much foundation, believed that Narendra Modi would play that role). The vocabulary of Indian politics remains overwhelmingly that introduced during the 1980s—reservations, religious rights, subsidies, and agriculture remain very much the bread and butter of political contest. The only real area of contestation that has been added to these issues is the struggle against displacement and land acquisition, which is also opposed to the interests of big capital. The change from the 1980s is in the disconnection between this political contestation and its ability to influence *policy*—but that does not make this politics irrelevant.

As a result, every time India's "economic reforms" policy advocates and their backers have had to face off against an organised political force, they have lost. Since 1991, certain "big" reforms have continuously been talked about but are nowhere near being implemented. These include the dismantling of the public distribution system (the 'ration' system), implementation of a "hire and fire" policy for industrial workers, privatisation of state-owned banks, total privatisation of public sector units, and capital account convertibility. On each of these policies, Congress and BJP governments have both tried steps in that direction and then been forced to hastily retreat when confronted with organised opposition.

As a result, India's "reformists" have only been able to get what they wanted through the backdoor. Thus the PDS system has been crippled with the introduction of "targeting", state-owned banks have been undercut by a combination of forced bad loans and the destruction of their role as social lenders, labour laws have been mangled by non-implementation, and so on. But the open political victory that was sought has never been achieved. Hence, as far back as 1999, the author Rob Jenkins[5] described India's reforms process as "reforms by stealth."

But this was not only a failure of the corporate-reformist political project—it was also a failure of the alliance between that project and Hindutva. Nothing symbolised that failure more than the infamous "India Shining" slogan that the BJP used in the 2004 general elections, which even today, over a decade later, is cited as an example of a delusional political campaign. "India Shining" sought to portray India as growing, developing and becoming stronger under the NDA government that ruled between 1998 and 2004 (with

5. Jenkins 1999.

the implicit subtext, of course, that if your life wasn't shining, perhaps you were not truly Indian). At the time almost the entire press effectively endorsed this picture as well. The election defeat that followed demonstrated that neither the RSS, nor Hindutva, nor "reforms" had anywhere near the popular support their supporters imagined that they had.

More importantly, they had been defeated by precisely the forces that—in their own *self-understanding*—they were supposed to have rendered irrelevant. Election surveys showed that neither "secularism" nor an explicit rejection of economic reforms had driven the NDA's defeat.[6] Rather, regional parties that had inherited the popular base of the 1980s movements; caste-based formations; politicians promising improved welfare entitlements; opposition from minority and marginalised communities; farmers angry with constant price volatility; these became the basis of the UPA's upset victory. All of these were politics that were not "developmental" or "nationalist" in the way that the RSS-corporate alliance defined those terms. Almost two decades after the onset of the mobilisations of the 1980s, the 2004 elections demonstrated that even six years of Sangh-driven government were not enough to destroy this politics.

For the Indian corporate sector this presented a major problem[7]. On the one hand, no clear political alternative emerged in 2004. As a result, their power remained largely intact and was under no serious threat. On the other, their agenda remained incomplete. In the first years of

6. See the nuanced and instructive discussion in Yadav 2004. He also points out that, had there been any political platform that had in fact made economic reforms a central issue, it is likely that they would have received considerable popular support. But the fact that this wasn't the case meant that the election did not revolve around this issue.

7. This issue is discussed in more detail in Gopalakrishnan 2013, and parts of this discussion are excerpted from there.

the United Progressive Alliance government, the Congress then attempted to manage this contradictory situation by implementing "globalisation with a human face." On the one hand, this meant continuing pro-corporate reforms. On the other, institutions like the National Advisory Council and the alliance with the Left parties were meant to make it possible to concede fundamental, long-term demands relating to social oppression—such as rural employment, forest rights, and so on—without directly threatening the big capitalists. In practice this approach did in fact work, and it won the Congress the 2009 elections. But just before that, the 2008 financial crisis hit.

Corporate capital's allegiance to this kind of hybrid politics was always weak, and after the global collapse of finance, it turned decisively against the UPA's politics. By 2011 every business paper in India was complaining of "policy paralysis"—by which they meant that the UPA was not capable of the kind of openly pro-corporate politics they sought. The Congress, unlike the RSS and the Sangh Parivar, is an incoherent formation without effective discipline or any clear ideology. Faced with this kind of pressure, it collapsed into ideological chaos and a "lame duck" government that simply lurched from one crisis to another. No major policy initiative other than a crippled Food Security Act was even attempted in the five years of the second UPA government.

With the death of that alternative, the Sangh's ideological attraction reasserted itself. That attraction manifested itself in the adulation that, from 2012 onwards, big business and the English press began to lavish on Narendra Modi. On the face of it, the Gujarat government had done nothing to warrant the kind of admiration it began to receive. In most respects, Gujarat actually fell in the middle of India's large states. Maharashtra and Karnataka (out of large states) had received more foreign direct investment. Even corporates seemed to have their doubts. Notwithstanding enormous publicity to the "Vibrant Gujarat" investor summits, even in the first one in 2003, only 57% of the promised investment was actually made. In every subsequent summit, it declined, from 57% to 35% to 23% to 8% to 1% in the 2013 one. Corporates were simply not putting their money where their mouth was.

As for the Gujarat government's 'development' achievements, they too were solidly mediocre. The Modi government's most often cited success was supposed rural electrification, but the 2011 Census showed that fifteen other states had a higher rate of electrified households than Gujarat—including Tamil Nadu, Haryana, Karnataka, Kerala and Punjab. In terms of "clean and effective administration", the CAG had twice indicted the Gujarat government for providing favours, and the Modi government had infamously tried to render the State Lokayukta completely toothless. Even in terms of GDP growth rates, ranked from 2002—2011, Gujarat came fourth. This is apart from the fact that the 2011 Human Development Report placed Gujarat at the eleventh position in human development, behind Tamil Nadu, Haryana, Maharashtra and Punjab. Finally, supporters often cited the fact that Modi had won three consecutive elections, but even among his contemporaries he was hardly unique in that respect; at the time, so had Naveen Patnaik, Tarun Gogoi, Sheila Dikshit, Manik Sarkar and Pawan Chamling.

Despite all this, a full-throated campaign soon became underway in the media and across all forms of communication portraying the successes of the "Gujarat model of development" and the unique efficiency of the Modi administration. Only two factors really distinguished Gujarat from other states. One was the 2002 killings and the manner in which Modi and his government appeared to somehow have converted this terrible mass slaughter into a *selling point* of their administration. The second was the clear domination of the Sangh and the BJP over all other forms of politics and organising in the state. Within a year of Modi taking power at the Centre, the hollowness of that domination had been exposed by the successive Patidar and Dalit mobilisations in the state. But in 2012 and 2013, the Sangh control of Gujarat appeared complete.

In other words, still in pursuit of an imaginary India where there is no collective mobilisation, Indian capitalists saw the Gujarat regime as a *successful* implementation of what they had been attempting for so long. Meanwhile, the crippled second UPA government continuously failed to address any of the significant welfare crises plaguing India's urban poor and rural areas, creating a miniature replay of the collapse of Congress hegemony in the 1980s. The resulting anti-corruption mobilisations were not of Sangh manufacture, but they provided the perfect atmosphere for a return of its politics. The individualist bargain offered to each of its cadres was now offered to the nation as a whole—give up struggles for rights and welfare, and accept the "honest" and "decent" leadership of the wise and the powerful, in exchange for security and prosperity. This is the oldest right wing formula in the world, and with the support of both capital and many of those left adrift by India's economy, it worked.

# 6
# May 2014 and After

When the BJP won a majority in Parliament in May 2014, its victory seemed to mark the triumph of RSS politics—after decades of trying, its ideas had finally swept the country. At the time that this is being written, we are roughly in the middle of this government's first five year term. In many ways, what was feared about a Sangh-driven government is already coming true, with everything from administrative appointments, to educational institutions, to foreign policy being driven by Hindutva ideological precepts.

But that is not quite the whole story. As the Sangh has grown, so have the problems—and the opposition—that it has to face. Now, the confrontation between the RSS and its various opponents has become the central question of Indian politics. We are at a crossroads in the history of both India and the Sangh. The next decade will have a crucial impact on the futures of both—and right now, the signs do not look promising for either.

In this book, I have sought to argue that the Sangh's impact is less about what it thinks it is trying to do, and more about the contradiction between that project and reality. Now that, for the first time in India's history, the Sangh actually has the power it has always craved, that contradiction is coming through in a more dramatic way than ever before.

## The Myopia Behind Sangh Strategy Under the Modi Government

If there is one point that both the Sangh's critics and supporters have always agreed upon, it is that the Sangh plans for the long term. Even staunch opponents will often—despairingly—talk of the Sangh's systematic operations over decades, arguing that the ability to do this is the key difference between it and all other political forces in India.

As we saw above, the RSS' ability to maintain a consistent strategy is indeed extraordinary. But this long term strategy hides a fundamental, deep-rooted *conceptual myopia*—and it is that side of the Sangh that is now coming to the fore. Achieving power has brought the RSS face to face with a familiar problem. It now has to deliver on its claims of being able to offer security and advancement to its base—and more importantly to its cadre—while simultaneously addressing the threats and challenges it faces to its dominance.

Of course, this is the dilemma faced by any political organisation that takes state power. But the RSS has a problem in addressing this dilemma that no other group faces—for both its ideology and its internal structure requires it to *act like these problems don't actually exist.*

In preceding chapters we saw how Hindutva blames all conflict on internal ignorance/weakness, on the one hand, and malign external interference on the other. Since the whole ideology is premised on the idea that conflict is both *evil* and *unnecessary*, its conceptual tools for dealing with real conflict are very limited. Only one strategy is available: first, decide if the opponent is 'internal' or 'external'; and second, 'educate' the internal opponents through coercive propaganda while crushing the external ones. Doing anything else means risking internal coherence, since acknowledging that democracy and mutual debate have a place in society means that they also should have a place within the Sangh Parivar.

The basic problem the RSS faces is that neither of these options—"education" or repression—works when there is a genuine contradiction of interests between it and forces that it cannot crush. This is precisely what is happening in various forms in India. At the time of writing—late 2016—contemporary events offer several obvious examples of this. The examples are likely to keep changing, but the basic tendency they illustrate is not.

The first and most striking is the biggest policy step the Modi government has taken so far—the "demonetisation" of Rs. 500 and Rs. 1,000 notes on November 8, 2016. That night, 86% of the cash in India (by value) became worthless. All of that cash had to be deposited or exchanged in banks. The justification given by the government (initially) was that the measure would tackle black money, or funds for which tax had not been paid.

At the time that this manuscript was being finalised—January 2017—the consequences of this drastic move are still playing out. But it is already clear that, for the agricultural, informal and unorganised sectors, the impact was devastating.

The full range of havoc that demonetisation wreaked is out of our scope here. Reports from around the country included closure of wholesale vegetable markets, market crashes for fresh produce that resulted in farmers throwing their vegetables on streets in protests, hundreds of thousands of migrant workers losing work and a large proportion facing starvation, loss of savings by working class women (less than a fifth of Indian women have their own bank accounts), and a massive impact on small industries and enterprises (India's largest manufacturers' association estimated[1] that its members had lost 35% of their revenues and 50% of their revenues). All of this occurred in an environment where the government's lack of seriousness about actual tax evasion became apparent. No action was taken against corporate tax evaders. Tax raids yielded only small totals of cash, but, strikingly, a large proportion of this was in the new notes that were issued to replace the old ones. This established that demonetisation did not even halt the cash hoarding that was the ostensible target of the entire exercise.[2]

A full discussion of the features and consequences of demonetisation, and the economic agendas that may have been its real purpose, is out of our scope here. But for all its unprecedented character as an *economic* measure, as a *political* measure demonetisation had all the hallmarks of a Sangh campaign—in its conception, in its execution, and in its trajectory over time.

Demonetisation was presented to the public as an exercise in mass political participation—cheerfully accept the loss to your livelihood (and in some cases your life) from demonetisation, as part of a national "movement" against individual "enemies" who are destroying society by hiding money. In November and December 2016, BJP leaders also repeatedly promised that demonetisation would yield a massive increase in tax receipts (and a "windfall" from unreturned cash, on which more below), and this would be distributed to the "poor." In other words, by choosing to cheerfully give up one's own economic rights and autonomy, one can gain a material benefit from the powerful—exactly the same bargain that the Sangh has always offered, as discussed in Chapter 4. Moreover, as

1. Janardhanan 2017.
2. For further discussion on this point, and sources for much of this information, please see Gopalakrishnan 2016a.

in all Sangh bargains, the element of both "choice" and participation were actually illusory—no one had any choice in the matter, and there was no meaningful participation that resulted from this forced destruction.

In this sense, demonetisation was the most successful Sangh Parivar campaign so far, since it reached practically every Indian household simultaneously. Moreover, the question of who is the "enemy" could be flexibly defined by the government itself—as a result of which no one, neither government nor opposition, chose to mention corporate tax evaders, while much publicity was given to minor income tax raids.[3]

But demonetisation also appears to have reached its comeuppance sooner than expected—since the gains promised have also turned out to be entirely illusory. This is discussed further in the next section.

Much the same structural features play themselves out in other Sangh/BJP campaigns after 2014. A second example is the ongoing contest for control over universities. Since the Modi government came to power in 2014, the Akhil Bharatiya Vidyarthi Parishad (ABVP) has systematically tried to provoke conflict in universities across India (JNU and Hyderabad Central University being the most prominent examples, but far from the only ones). Each attack has followed an identical template. The ABVP targets some event or public statement by Ambedkarite, Dalit and Left organisations as 'anti national'. This allegation is then converted into a violent clash, either by the ABVP's cadre physically attacking their opponents and/or by the university administration taking action against the left or Dalit group at the behest of the Centre (which immediately jumps in to support the ABVP, contrary to all normal

3. This point is discussed in Gopalakrishnan 2016b.

precedents of the way universities are run). Once this occurs, the police inevitably get involved; and once again, given the support of the Centre, the police tend to connive with the ABVP. The ABVP then uses the combined force of its cadre and the police to try to crush its opponents in the crudest manner possible, using arrests, violence and harassment through police cases. At the time of writing, one student in JNU—Najeeb Ahmad—has simply disappeared after being assaulted by ABVP cadre.

The same pattern, again, is visible in the rapid deterioration of the political situation in Kashmir. The political dynamics of the Kashmir conflict are of course far more complex than the Sangh's role alone, and are outside my scope here. Indeed, by and large BJP-Sangh rule has simply continued what previous governments have done, and on Kashmir almost all parties have identical positions in any case. But the RSS' influence is visible in two facets. The first is the deliberate stoking of violence, blockades and open discrimination in the Jammu region, which has reached unprecedented levels in the past five years. The second is the increased ferocity with which the Central government has met Kashmiris' protests after the killing of Burhan Wani in June 2016. In 2016 the Kashmir valley was under curfew for longer than ever in its history. More than 1,800 people were detained under the State's draconian Public Safety Act—more than was even the case at the height of the violence in the early 1990s.[4]

Moreover, rather than respond to the spiraling protests, the Central government sought in August 2016 to turn attention to the conflict in Balochistan—making thinly veiled threats that India would support Baloch rebels if Pakistan did not stop supporting Kashmiri groups. Then, after the September 2016 attack on an army base in Uri,

4. Masood 2016.

the central government launched public "surgical strikes" across the Line of Control—the details of which remain very murky—while publicly boasting that it had attacked "terrorist launchpads." Violence at the Line of Control then escalated to levels that have not been seen since the 2003 ceasefire, with more firing incidents recorded in October 2016 than in the entirety of the preceding year. Meanwhile, within India, there was a massive increase in war rhetoric. As I wrote the first draft of this, a public TV nearby was playing a ticker loop asking "Kya Pakistan ke liye yudd hi ilaaz hai?"[5]

A final example is the "cow protection" movement. The rise of violent *gau rakshak* (cow protection) groups since May 2014 is massive and unprecedented. Across every state in north and central India, such gangs are now active, engaging in extortion, torture and killings in the name of stopping animal slaughter. The targets of the violence are almost exclusively Muslims and Dalits, though in reality corporations owned by Jains and high caste Hindus are among the biggest beef traders; and elite establishments serving beef have never been targeted. In all these states the police have connived with the violence. The states of Haryana and Gujarat have announced that they will give these groups semi-official status with cards declaring them to be "protection volunteers," and both States have set up separate official bodies for the purpose of promoting cow protection. These *gau rakshak* organisations have flaunted their closeness with the Centre and State governments, openly circulating gruesome torture videos and declaring themselves to be nationalists. In one particularly egregious incident, after a *gau rakshak* cadre accused of murdering Mohammed Akhlaq died, his funeral bier was draped in the Indian flag with a Central Minister in attendance.

5. "Is war the only cure for Pakistan?"

## The Playing Out of Contradictions

At first glance these examples all seem to show the Sangh's success. For all the devastation that demonetisation has caused, almost three months after the decision, opinion polls still indicate that a significant portion of the population describe it as a "good move". Protests against it have been widespread but relatively muted, and even the opposition parties are no longer raising it at the national level (though they have continued to do so in election campaigns). English media outlets periodically publish articles trying to explain why there is not more protest.

Meanwhile, the ABVP is winning most of its clashes; its rivals are either being expelled or subject to such harassment that their activities are greatly reduced. War hysteria about Pakistan has stayed at very high levels, and completely swept away any public discussion about the brutal crackdown in Kashmir. The 'surgical strikes' were an unqualified propaganda success, bringing an image of RSS-style 'strength' and 'character' to the BJP and the government that the vast majority of the media openly promoted. Meanwhile, the gau rakshaks continue to expand, and no State or Central institution has shown any inclination to confront them. Anyone engaged in trade related to cows today lives in a climate of intense fear.

But these superficial 'successes' overlook certain deeper problems. Each of these moves has faced resistance in multiple forms—and that resistance has defeated the stated agenda of the move.

Demonetisation, as noted above, has so far not delivered any meaningful gain to anyone other than big corporates who received a windfall from lower bank interest rates (a result of the massive amounts of cash deposited in banks). Rumours of money being distributed to the poor; of free rations under the Food Security Act; of new 'big bang' welfare schemes; all have come to nought in the 2017 Union budget (released as I'm finalising this manuscript). The fundamental reason for this is that the government had been anticipating that much of the demonetised cash would simply not make its way to banks—a reasonable expectation, given both some tax evaders and the number of poor, sick and marginalised people who would not have been able to do so. This unreturned cash would then be 'extinguished' through a law, meaning that the Reserve Bank of India could effectively hand over the value of that cash to the government. But reports now indicate that 97% of the cash was returned.[6] As a result, in the Union Budget for 2017—2018, no gain for the vast majority of the population was announced—only routine adjustments in tax slabs. The BJP government, following Sangh principles, essentially underestimated the "enemy" it claimed to be tackling (those hoarding cash to evade tax). These 'enemies' easily escaped the "national movement" against them, as nothing was done to actually tackle the structures of tax evasion. Meanwhile, as discussed below, demonetisation has undermined the entire Indian economy.

The fact is that neither the Sangh nor the BJP government has any workable method of *resolving* these issues in their favour—or, indeed, resolving them in any way at all. Each of these conflicts is creating fallout that is rapidly growing beyond the capacity of the government to manage.

In the case of Kashmir, expectations have been created within the country by the government's rhetoric about Balochistan and 'striking' Pakistan, neither of which it has any capacity to carry out. Meanwhile, the collapse of peace and the ratcheting up of tensions has forced international attention to return to the conflict. No major power in the area—whether Russia, China or the US—has any interest

6. Singh and Pradhan 2017.

in permitting a serious India-Pakistan conflict, and all will act in concert to stop any such development. In this sense the only near term resolution this conflict is likely to see will be one imposed from outside, most likely by the US. Will such a compromise fit within the Sangh's ideology? That remains to be seen.

In the case of the other two conflicts, the mafia-like behaviour of both the ABVP and the *gau rakshak* groups has triggered widespread political resistance. The ABVP's offensives have not earned it victories in elections in the universities where it has attacked other groups. The suicide of Rohit Vemula in Hyderabad Central University triggered a nationwide backlash from Dalit and left groups that the Modi government has seemed almost incapable of handling. *Gau rakshak* violence has resulted in mass Dalit protests in Gujarat, one of the largest political mobilisations the State has seen in recent times, as well as widespread Dalit resistance to the Sangh. Reports say that attendance at specially-created "Dalit shakhas" in UP dropped massively in the wake of the torture of Dalits by gau rakshaks in Una.[7] Meanwhile, following the attacks, the Bahujan Samaj Party has begun openly advocating a Muslim-Dalit alliance in Uttar Pradesh; whether that alliance fructifies in the 2017 state election or not, such openly anti Hindutva rhetoric by a large party has a long term political impact. In perhaps the best example of the Sangh's panicky response to these conflicts, PM Modi declared in August 2016 that "70%-80% of these [cow protection] groups are criminals"—but, since all gau rakshak groups are led by Sangh Parivar cadre, this implies that the same proportion of Sangh cadre are criminals. Naturally, this remark provoked howls of protest from the VHP and a rebuke from the RSS sarsanghchalak.

7. See Jha 2016.

Where each of these conflicts will go is impossible to predict. The Sangh may yet succeed in finding ways to maintain them for years to come. But the essential truth that they reveal remains—the Sangh is only capable of exacerbating these problems. The Sangh's claim to stability thus essentially reduces to saying that it can fight these conflicts more effectively than anyone else. But that only works for a while—because it is not, at any level, capable of either *ending* or *winning* them.

## The Alliance With Corporates and Big Capital

The 2014 election victory did not belong to the Sangh alone. The open promotion of Narendra Modi and the BJP by all of India's companies and corporate-owned media outlets contributed greatly to this victory; indeed, this media support was probably more responsible for the scale of the victory than the RSS' own groundwork and campaigning. In chapters 3 and 5, the possible logics of this alliance between capital and the Sangh were discussed, and two basic common agendas emerged between these forces. The first and deeper one was the desire of both forces to finish off the collective and community-based politics that continues to dominate the Indian political landscape. The second and more immediate agenda was the search by India's big capitalists for a political force that could ensure political stability for its policy changes, while deflecting or crushing resistance to them.

But the problem that India's corporate sector faces parallels that of the RSS—it actually has no ability to achieve either of these objectives, *even* in alliance with the Sangh. It has found itself incapable of addressing the basic contradictions of a "reformed" economy. These contradictions have manifested themselves in two major forms, both of which are not unique to India but shared by economies across the globe. Discussing these problems in detail would require a book of its own; hence I have given very brief summaries here, along with references for further reading.

The first contradiction that occurs in "reformed" economies is the collapse of demand because of stagnation in the incomes of the majority of people. Without income, people cannot buy products, and hence producers cannot sell them. India's economy, with its huge population of desperately poor people, has always suffered from this problem. But the resulting demand crunch has deepened considerably in the last three years.[8] One key reason for is that, particularly since 2014, redistribution and welfare schemes that provide a basic safety net for people have been subject to systematic cuts. The Mahatma Gandhi National Rural Employment Guarantee Act—the world's largest employment generation programme—has seen severe funding cuts. As a result, in 2014 and 2015, rural wages grew at a slower rate than they had at any time in the previous decade.[9] With such severe stagnation of demand, investments too have fallen.[10] Companies find little reason to invest money when there is little chance of either profits from sales or being able to recover their investment. Demonetisation has meanwhile depressed demand much more, leading to a further slide in credit offtake in November and December 2016.

Rather than allow for these problems to be addressed, Indian corporates have turned to pressuring the government to hand over public resources—particularly natural resources—to them. Such moves, intensifying since 2000, allow these companies to earn quick profits by speculating

8. *The Economist* 2016.

9. *Scroll.in* 2015.

10. ENS 2016.

on or selling off these resources—without worrying too much about producing things for the consumer market.[11] This trend has had two further negative consequences. First, it led to the explosion of giant scams in the latter years of the UPA government, all of which involved the Central government facilitating resource grabbing by select corporates. Second, it can at most benefit only a small fraction of India's companies, since the majority have neither the financial muscle nor the political clout to engage in this kind of profiteering. With no demand, falling investment, and rampant speculation, corporates lose the ability to repay their loans, leading finally to the biggest problem facing the Indian economy today—the banking crisis created by ballooning loan defaults.

The second contradiction manifested in the 2008 financial crisis. Confronting exactly the same problem at the global level—stagnating incomes leading to ever higher debt spirals—the global financial sector collapsed in a spectacular fashion. At the time of writing, most industrial economies have not fully recovered from this crisis. In India the public banking sector buffered the country's economy from immediate catastrophe, but the crisis manifested itself as a reluctance to invest by foreign capitalists—and a political swing by Indian capitalists against any form of public spending that did not immediately benefit them, as discussed in the last chapter. This is what led to the attacks on welfare schemes after 2010.

Both of these contradictions, but particularly the first one, have led to the essential political weakness of the "reforms" project in India. The result has been a cycle of efforts to push through more "reforms" and repeated political defeats, as we discussed in the last chapter. But this cycle has not just slowed down reforms as such—

11. See Gopalakrishnan 2015 for a more detailed discussion of this point.

it has resulted in a fundamental change in the project itself.

For, just as with the Sangh, the key fact here is not that this problem exists but that its authors, the corporate sector, are *intellectually bereft of any ability to deal with it.* Having failed to achieve any of their big dreams, they have—instead of revising those dreams—simply started dressing up more and more short term, knee jerk policies as "reforms." This becomes apparent if one examines what these lobbies and their intellectuals are now pushing. Several of these initiatives have been apparent since 2014.

The first of these pushes was for 'reform' of labour laws; most pro-corporate commentators cite the Rajasthan government's dilution of the Industrial Disputes Act's clauses on closure of factories as a "major step forward" and "hire and fire" as the key method to ensuring employment generation. But these clauses actually affect only a tiny minority of India's companies—a reporter in Rajasthan found that companies have never had much trouble with these sections, and in fact most of them are not even aware that these laws exist[12]. Given this, "reforms" in labour law are essentially irrelevant to any question of employment.[13] Politically, after the 2014 hype about the Rajasthan government's move, this agenda has largely vanished from public debate.

The second reformist attempt was the abortive attempt to force through an amendment to the Land Acqusition Act in 2015, which failed in the face of a national movement uniting opposition parties, social movements and farmers' organisations in defending the need for consent prior to acquisition of land. Several State governments—Gujarat first among them—have passed the same amendment since, in

12. Sharma 2014.

13. Roychowdhury 2014.

the name of accelerating "reforms". But once again, such efforts address 'problems' affecting only a small fraction of India's companies, essentially those engaged in extractive industries and those speculating with land and natural resources. Moreover, these companies have mostly had little trouble with accessing these resources in any case, as discussed above.[14]

Finally, there are calls to privatise public sector banks as a way to address the bad loans crisis. This flies in the face of evidence that it was the public sector character of these banks that prevented the financial crisis from being *worse*, as well as international evidence that private banks are more prone to speculation and irresponsible lending than public ones. Privatisation will both worsen India's credit crisis and deprive the government of its only instrument for intervening in the financial sector—and for the latter reason it is unlikely that it will happen in any case.

The result of all of this is that, at the time of writing, every economic index—except the government's somewhat dubious GDP statistics—has been sliding downwards. Exports, demand and investment are all declining.[15]

Then, in such a situation, the government undertook demonetisation—a political move driven by the RSS' ideological precepts. In one stroke this exacerbated literally every one of the Indian economy's major problems—the crunch in demand, the ripple effect creating the bad loans' crisis, falling exports, etc. In this sense demonetisation has massively undercut all the BJP government's own stated economic goals. But, in a sign of the same intellectual bankruptcy, a significant number of pro BJP economists did a complete 180 degree turn on their own stands and

14. Gopalakrishnan 2015.

15. Jain 2016.

supported the move; even in the face of criticism from both left wing and right wing economists from other countries. And India's corporate sector, ever the venal cowards, either remained silent or praised the move. Only the small number of indebted large corporations benefited from demonetisation—which led to lower interest rates— and even they are likely to suffer from the resulting demand crunch. Both the economic incoherence and the political hollowness of Indian neoliberalism were exposed in a single policy.

Again, this does not mean that India's economy is necessarily going to collapse or enter some kind of major recession, though the latter is possible. Rather, the most significant aspect of this development is that India's two most powerful forces—the Sangh and its corporate allies—are reaching the limits of their political projects.

Their alliance, intended to cement and consolidate the power of both, is instead eroding the power of both. India's corporates have always been unconcerned with conflict or violence, and in that sense the spiraling violence triggered by the Sangh is not a problem as such for them. But today they find themselves saddled with an unreliable political ally which does not seem to be able to deliver the guaranteed political victories that it had promised. Moreover, it is not delivering the 'reforms' they seek either—however limited those reforms might be.

Simultaneously, the Sangh finds that its promise to its base, and to India generally, of jobs and higher incomes—a translated policy version of its individualist bargain—is not delivering either. It has no coherent vision of the economy, and now its allies don't have one either. It is left only with the need to continually create more conflict in order to consolidate its own base. This is the dead end in which all majoritarian and fascist forces eventually find themselves—and the Sangh is barreling towards it at an ever faster pace.

## Implications for the State and Wider Politics

These developments are not just a problem for these two forces alone. One of the features of a successful political project is that it also successfully "explains" the world to *its own beneficiaries,* namely the powerful, in an effective and useful manner. Those in power often see the world through the lenses of the same ideological project that they seek to convince the rest of the population to believe. If the reformist-Hindutva marriage is growing incapable of *explaining* social conflict to its proponents, and those proponents are hence drifting into incoherence, myopia and confusion, this has implications for India as a whole.

This problem is not unique to the post 2014 period. From almost the time of the first NDA regime, the drift of India's capitalists towards short term initiatives and profiteeering has gradually meant that the state machinery has lost any sense of coherent policy goals. As a result, both state and Central governments have increasingly moved to shorter and shorter term initiatives.

After the NDA's defeat in 2004, this tendency reversed for a brief period. The then new United Progressive Alliance government—unsure of its own footing and only aware that it needed to look beyond "reforms" for popularity—attempted a new compromise, as discussed in chapter 5. For the brief period that it lasted, this attempt provided the policy space for a few more long term initiatives, namely the so-called "rights based" legislations discussed in that chapter. But with the closing of that space, policy making rapidly fell back into short term incoherence.

Meanwhile, at the State government level, this drift was already well underway. Increasingly, State governments have turned to visible, concrete welfare schemes in order to generate popularity. The best known of these have been the distribution of free goods—laptops, cycles, mobile phones, TVs—in state after state (Tamil Nadu being a pioneer in this regard). This kind of institutionalised patronage—while far from irrelevant to people's needs—has been accompanied by a near complete absence of both *intellectual* and *political* initiatives capable of responding to India's severe institutional and economic crisis. The only partial exception to this was the rise of the Aam Aadmi Party, which soon also began to drift into the same style of action. Accompanying this process has been the rise to dominance of symbolic, leader centred politics in state after state.

After the BJP came to power in 2014, given the myopia of both the RSS and its corporate allies, this kind of politics is now being replicated at the national level. New 'schemes' are being launched frequently, with slogan-style names ("Jan Dhan Yojana", Swach Bharat Abhiyan, Stand Up India Start Up India, etc.). But most of these schemes are either rehashed versions of earlier minor schemes or irrelevant to all but a small minority.

On the policy front, there are now no strong policies visible in either direction—towards greater distributionism or towards greater power to capitalists. Instead, there are project-oriented decisions taken to appease particular corporates or particular agencies, with each policy being made on the basis of a short term calculation of immediate benefit to someone. As a result, Narendra Modi's own party peers have derided him as an event manager rather than a serious policymaker. Demonetisation was perhaps the most glaring example of such a policy.

In short, the cul de sac that the Sangh and corporates find themselves in is amplifying and accelerating a crisis for Indian politics in general. For all its much vaunted long term strategy, what the Sangh is actually delivering today is a descent into incoherence and contradiction—underlaid and built upon a foundation of violence.

# 7

# Trends and Trajectories

This book has tried to examine the implications of the growth of the Sangh Parivar—for itself, for other Indians and for Indian politics in general. In a whistle-stop tour of history, the book has looked at the RSS' ideas, at its social and political roots, at the circumstances that have led to its rise, and at the dead end which both it and the country are rapidly reaching.

One question remains: what might happen now?

Prediction is always a dangerous game in a book about politics—especially when the situation is so fluid, changing almost every day. However, as the book has explored, the saffron-corporate alliance that today runs India is the culmination of a number of long-term processes that have brought us to this point. Looking at where those processes are headed might help us identify the strongest *tendencies* in the current situation.

As discussed in the last chapter, both of these forces now have more power than they have ever had before—and simultaneously have less of an idea about how to *use* that power than ever before. In the case of the corporate sector, the effect of this has been to render them ever more myopic and narrow in their focus. In the case of the Sangh, we can expect a similar effect—but with several complex dynamics coming into play.

The RSS' ideology focuses on individual character, and its organisational structure is built around cadre who understand their own security and value as resulting only from their importance to those above them. Both of these tendencies result in a very difficult situation for the organisation if it begins to fail. In the last chapter we saw how the RSS' lack of conceptual tools for understanding social conflict is leading it into cul de sac after cul de sac. But this also means that it has no tools for understanding failure. If there is failure, in the RSS' worldview, it must be the fault of some individual. For many cadre, the natural interpretation would be that someone above them has sold out or betrayed the cause. Much like the old Communist left, every historical shift and every setback to the cause will be seen as a conspiracy abetted by some insider.

And now, given its power and dominance, for the first time in its history, the Sangh Parivar faces the real, genuine possibility of *failure*. As its critics keep reminding it, there is no one left to blame now. This is one reason why everyone in the Modi government, from Ministers to social media trolls, is so anxious to constantly say that they are in any case better than the Congress, or if they are failing, it is only because of the Congress—making them sound like whiny teenagers rather than leaders of a ruling party. But this can only go on for so long.

At the end of the day cadre will begin to ask where the stability, security and dominance they were promised are, and why the organisation seems to be leading them into more insecurity rather than less. At that point a gradual process of splintering is likely to begin to occur, with new factions coming up that each promise to be more radical and more 'honest' than the last. This process is familiar from similar groups in other countries. Pakistan is a classic example—with the increasing power of Islamist far right groups, and the failure of those groups to achieve their goals, the result has been that new factions have come up and literally gone to war both with the state and with each other. In the Middle East, the clash between Al Qaeda and ISIS exhibits a similar dynamic.

There are some small indicators of this splintering already happening with the RSS—indeed, from prior to 2014 as well. Recent years have seen the rise of groups like Abhinav Bharat and the Sanatan Sanstha, both of whom have allegedly undertaken bombing and assassination campaigns while accusing the RSS of being 'soft'. But such minor fissures are a long way from a total breakdown, of course. The loose hierarchy of the Sangh Parivar structure allows for a certain level of internal dissent without resulting in collapse. Moreover, the Sangh has only been in power for a very short time. Its resilience will be tested more in the years to come, particularly if the BJP manages to win the 2019 general elections.

If the coherence of the Sangh Parivar does begin to break down, the implications for the rest of India would probably depend on two factors. The first would be the speed and nature of the breakdown. Will the new factions be more violent? Will they ally with existing non-RSS forces like the Shiv Sena, or set out on their own? Will they choose to attack the RSS itself? All of these questions cannot be answered at present. They will have serious implications for the amount of bloodshed and chaos that might result.

But it is the other factor that will be decisive. That factor is the response of the forces in Indian society that are *opposed* to the RSS and to Hindutva.

There is, of course, a range of such forces today. These include large sections of the regional parties; parts of the Congress; the communist Left; the non-party 'progressive democratic' movements; large parts of the student movement; the Muslim right; progressive Muslim organisations; the Dalit movement; much of the workers' movement; the various separatist and 'subnational' movements; the women's movement; and so on. Each of these forces deserves a book of its own, and I will not be discussing them here. But the rise of the Sangh Parivar creates certain political circumstances that have implications for all of these movements, and for many other Indians besides.

The 2014 campaign to bring the BJP to power brought together practically all the most powerful forces in Indian society. We have already seen the attraction it held for India's big capitalists, and the resultant media adulation the Modi campaign received. These capitalists were joined by the powerful purveyors of modern-day 'traditional culture' (defined essentially by casteism and patriarchy), personified by people like Sri Sri Ravi Shankar and Baba Ramdev. On top of this coalition came the indirect or open support of 'military experts', 'security experts', retired intelligence officials and others whose views are generally taken to represent those in the security forces and the military.

In other words, in 2014, most of India's casteist, patriarchal, repressive, and exploitative forces threw their lot in with the BJP in a spectacularly public fashion. As we saw in chapters 3 and 5, this was not an accident, but rather a reflection of long term political trends—as well as of the failure of these forces to find any other political 'home' as congenial as this one.

But this also means that the nexus of power relations that underlie so much of Indian politics has been exposed by 2014 as never before. If this makes it clear who is on the side of the RSS, it also makes it clear who is not. This has two fundamental implications for the opposition.

First, it obviously makes it easier to unite. Halfway into the Modi government's rule this is already widely apparent. Whereas earlier an assault on JNU students would have generated outrage only on the left, today it is both easy and necessary for everyone to link the dots, with this assault being seen as one part of a generalised attack on minorities, democratic rights and freedom of expression—by the Sangh and the state together. The suicide of a Dalit student, Rohit Vemula, triggers outrage not only from the Dalit movement but from the left, several regional parties and even parts of the mainstream media.

The second implication is, however, perhaps more important. Exposing these power structures means that resistance also has the chance to become deeper—more *radical,* in the true meaning of the word.[1] The link between big business, the media and the RSS is, for instance, now accepted by an ever larger section of public opinion. The RSS' links with casteism were earlier a leftist epithet hurled at the organisation; today they are central to the campaigns of several regional parties. The link between corporate exploitation, RSS ideology and threats to basic freedoms have also become a part of the public common sense.

Both these factors combined can lead, ideally, to new forms of resistance emerging that transcend older boundaries and also bring in new sections. The first glimmerings of this can already be seen in Indian politics.

One small but significant example was the *award wapsi* movement of 2015—when dozens of Indian writers returned their Sahitya Akademi literary awards in protest. This was unprecedented in Indian politics. These were writers across language, region and even ideology, united by their disgust at a government that turned a blind eye to the assassination

1. The word "radical", as the Radical Notes blog explains, is drawn from the Latin word radix—or root.

of progressive intellectuals and the growing *gau rakshak* violence across India.

Similarly, in 2016, we have seen the rise of the Dalit movement in Gujarat—in a state where Dalit politics had seemed invisible since 1985—and an explicit linkage by its leadership between caste violence and landlessness. The demand for land for Dalits is not a new one, but what is new is the sheer scale of the movement for this demand now.

Meanwhile, even as almost the entirety of TV media and large sections of the print media have turned into vocal RSS supporters, after 2014 there has been a small but disproportionately effective group of journalists who are directly exposing the RSS, corporates, casteism and violence. This has coincided with the new trend of news websites, some of which have almost made it their mission to highlight the 'marginalised'—whose interests are now, by definition, opposed to those of the RSS.

Finally, all of these trends lead in turn to an intense trend of *polarisation* where every incident is immediately seen in light of its long-range political implications. At the time of writing, for instance, the Central government has just imposed a one day ban on NDTV India for its coverage of the attacks on an air force base in Pathankot. A one day ban on a smaller news channel might earlier have attracted criticism. But at present it has generated an uproar like never before, with opposition politicians from Karunanidhi to Mamata Banerjee condemning the ban and street protests taking place across India.

All of this, of course, is far from posing any fundamental threat to either the RSS or Hindutva ideology. There is a very long way to go before that occurs. Consolidation and innovation are still the exception rather than the rule. Most of the resistance to the Sangh Parivar remains defensive and reactive. As a result, it still seems more likely than not that the BJP will win the 2019 general elections and the Modi government will continue for a decade. It is also highly likely that this government will use the same tactics that every authoritarian government in the world has used- creating a situation of economic or national crisis, perhaps through engineering violence or economic collapse, and thereby building a wave of fear in its favour (while justifying its repression of its opponents). Demonetisation was a potent example of this tactic, and the next round is likely to be even more intense. Such steps would prolong RSS-BJP rule for some time.

But none of these methods can work forever. The BJP's victory in 2014 has created the possibility of a genuinely new politics—and showed, also, that such a politics is necessary. The more powerful the Sangh Parivar grows, the more powerful these forces will grow too. The real question is whether the resulting possibilities will fructify—whether a genuine progressive alternative will emerge, overcoming its own internal tensions and contradictions. This does not need to be any single new party, or any single new force. It need only be something as vague as a new common sense.

If such an alternative were to emerge, the disintegration of the Sangh need not lead to a Pakistan-like situation of spiralling violence and collapse. It could lead to a new, more genuinely liberal India, a country witnessing genuine struggles against the injustice and the indignity that the Sangh perverts into support for Hindutva. It could be the start of something truly new.

All of this could happen. Will it? As of today, that question remains wide open.

In the ultimate analysis, the RSS and organisations of its ilk—wherever they have arisen in the world—represent the most malignant forms of political thought. From the Nazis to the Islamists to the Sangh Parivar, these groups promise security in exchange for giving up freedom; 'prosperity' in exchange for the loss of dignity; 'respect' in exchange for abandoning basic humanity. It is for that reason that they must be opposed. Not only because of 'secularism' or 'minority rights' or even 'freedom', but because they negate the very idea of *human dignity*. It is also for this reason that they have always failed, and will ultimately fail in India too. How and when they fail will decide how many innocent lives, and how much of this country's future, they will take with them. That is the challenge facing anyone committed to the ideals of democracy in India today.

# Appendix
# Some Myths About Muslims[1]

**Myth:** "'Muslim' countries are never secular. Muslims do not tolerate minorities in 'their' countries but demand minority rights in other countries."

The world's largest Muslim majority country is Indonesia (total population approximately 25 crores, larger than Pakistan). Indonesia is a secular democracy. Indeed, its population is almost a mirror image of India's—88% Muslim, 9% Christian, 3% Hindu, 2% Buddhist, etc. (as compared to India, which has a population that is 80% Hindu, 13.4% Muslim, 2.3% Christian, etc.) Indonesia's national slogan is "Unity in Diversity." Yes, Indonesia has riots and bomb blasts, but so does India.

In reality the majority of Muslim majority countries in the world are secular. Several large examples include Turkey, Mali, Syria, Niger, and Kazakhstan. Despite having Islam as 'state religion', Bangladesh's government is also secular in law. The same is true of many other countries. Only six countries in the world claim to use Islam as the basis of their law making—and their total population is roughly the same as the population of Indonesia, Turkey and Kazakhstan combined. In other words, the vast majority of Muslim majority countries are secular, and the vast majority of Muslims live under secular governments.

1. This is an updated version of a note published on *Kafila* in April 2014.

**Myth:** "Not all Muslims may be terrorists, but most terrorists are Muslims."

Even if we accept the government's definition of who is a terrorist in India, this is entirely untrue. In India, less than a third of the organisations banned as "terrorist" under the Unlawful Activities (Prevention) Act are Muslim organisations. Internationally, the group that engaged in the most suicide bombings in the world was the LTTE in Sri Lanka—a militantly atheist group whose members are mostly of Hindu and Christian origin.

It is also not true that Muslim organisations engage in the most violence in India. Between 2005 and 2014, as per the South Asia Terrorism Portal[2], twice as many people were killed in 'terrorist incidents' by Northeastern militant organisations and "left wing extremism". These are all non-Muslim organisations, and the largest Northeastern organisation in this period (ULFA) has a mostly Hindu, upper caste leadership.

Besides, the definition of "terrorism" that the government uses is contradictory. Killing twenty people by a bomb blast is considered terrorism, but the killing of thousands of people in 1984 or in Gujarat in 2002 (or, for that matter, the killing of 40 people in Muzaffarnagar, 68 people in Orissa in 2008, etc.) are not. All riots involve planning, stockpiling of weapons and systematic attacks. Why then are they not considered terrorism?

**Myth:** "Muslims have always been fundamentalists and are 'more religious' than followers of other religions."

Recent history shows that this is a lie, and also exposes where current "Muslim fundamentalism" comes from.

2. See here: http://www.satp.org/satporgtp/countries/india/database/Cumulative_Fatalities.htm

Just forty to sixty years ago, in most of the major regions of the world with high Islamic populations—Indonesia, the Middle East, north Africa—the strongest political forces were secular leftists. This took many forms: the Indonesian Communist Party; the Nasserite and Baa'thist regimes in Egypt, Syria and Iraq; the Iranian government of Mohammed Mossadegh, etc. In these countries, especially in the Middle East, the United States and its client states (such as Saudi Arabia) sponsored, financed and armed right wing and religious fundamentalist organisations, precisely in order to counter the strength of the secular leftists whom they opposed. Similarly, Israel's role in propping up Hamas to counter the Palestinian Liberation Organisation is also well known. This reached its height in the 1980s with the war in Afghanistan, with the US bankrolling and training the people who later founded Al Qaeda. US President Ronald Reagan famously called the fundamentalists of Afghanistan the equivalent of the founding fathers of the United States. It was during this period as well that the US financed and supported the Zia regime in Pakistan in its "Islamisation" drive. The current strength of the Islamic fundamentalist movement in the Middle East is a result of American strategy, which involved finishing off all leftist resistance while tolerating and encouraging Islamic fundamentalism.

Above all, to repeat the key point, Islamic fundamentalism is a *political* phenomenon created by a particular history—just like Hindutva, Christian fundamentalism and every other form of right wing movement. The myth of the inherently fundamentalist Muslim owes a lot to European mythmaking around the Crusades and subsequent efforts to prop up their empire in India. But people continue to recycle colonial self-justifications as if they are true.

**Myth:** "Muslims always start violence. Hindus only 'retaliate' or 'act in self-defence'."

Every single group that has ever engaged in mass killings has claimed to be 'retaliating' or 'defending themselves'.' The September 11 attacks in the US were justified as "retaliation" for the killing of lakhs of people in Iraq (through the crippling sanctions that followed the Gulf War) and the mass killing of civilians in Palestine by the US and Israel. If you believe the e-mails being sent before the Delhi and Ahmedabad bomb blasts in 2008, the blasts were "retaliation" for police atrocities and the massacre of Muslims in Gujarat. In 2008 Christians were massacred in Orissa in "retaliation" for the killing of a VHP leader. Going back further in history, the Nazis justified the *Kristallnacht*—their biggest state-sponsored riot against Jews, in which thousands of synagogues and homes were destroyed—by claiming it was "retaliation" for the murder of a German diplomat and necessary to 'defend themselves' against 'international Jewry'.

The reason this happens is simple—the only way to convince people to commit inhuman atrocities against other people is to make them believe that they are "defending themselves" or "paying back." These atrocities then become a justification for others to "retaliate" again. Thus the anti-Muslim killings of 1992 in Mumbai produced the bomb blasts of 1993 "in retaliation", leading to more killings in 1993, also "in retaliation", and so on and so forth. The sheer inhumanity of talking about "retaliation" is obvious. If Biharis formed a militia, should they be allowed to kill Maharashtrians to "defend themselves" against atrocities by the Shiv Sena? Should Northeast militant organisations go around massacring people in Delhi in "retaliation" for atrocities against Northeasterners in the capital? Would the same people who talk about how "Hindus only retaliate" then justify such atrocities as well? It is a mark of how low we have come as a society that so many people go around mouthing these slogans today, as if the gangrape of women and the murder of innocents (in so many riots) can ever be justified by "retaliation" and "self-defence."

**Myth:** "Hindus do not kill based on their religion. Only Muslims do, because their religion requires them to."

In Gujarat in 2002, in Delhi and other cities in 1984, in Bhagalpur in 1989, and in most other riots, the overwhelming majority of those who died were from minority communities (Muslims, Sikhs, etc.) Then we have the recent instances of bomb blasts by Hindutva organisations. The majority of the killers in all these incidents were Hindus, and the organisations that drove the killings called on them to kill non-Hindus. Would it be accurate to say they killed *because* Hinduism required them to do so? No, clearly, in all those instances, the attackers and the organisers were political groups seeking political goals (and dressing them up as religious goals). This is exactly what far right Muslim groups do too.

Every religion has groups that urge conflict with other religions, and holy texts in every religion contain things that endorse atrocities (just look at what the *Manu Smriti* says about women and Dalits, or the Old Testament of the Bible says about massacres of non-Jews). This does not mean that followers of those religions follow those texts literally. The vast majority of Muslims, like the vast majority of Hindus, Christians, or any other group, have never killed anyone and never will.

**Myth:** "Muslims are united and act together, while Hindus are divided and weak."

Every election study ever done has found that Muslims vote in the same manner as any other community votes—for facilities, on the basis of the candidate, whether they like a political party, etc. Muslims are no more united than any other group; they have internal divisions on religious, caste, gender, regional, language and countless other lines, just like any other community in India. If Muslims were "united", one would expect that they would be represented well in Parliament. In fact, Muslim MPs constituted only 5.5% of the 2009-2014 Lok Sabha, even though they are more than 13% of the population. In the May 2014 elections, their share dropped to 4.2%.

If anything, in today's cities the idea of "Muslims all live together" has been created by discrimination against them and them being forced to live in particular ghettos.

Meanwhile, in voting, people worry about their own physical safety. Just as a Bihari will not vote for a Shiv Sena candidate, most Muslims would not vote for the BJP. This is, once again, common sense. A party which has built itself by calling you foreigners, terrorists and anti-nationals is not likely to win your vote.

**Myth:** "The government favours Muslims and pampers them."

On the contrary, official data indicates systematic discrimination against Muslims. The Sachar Committee found that availability of bus stops, roads, bank branches and other basic infrastructure is lower in Muslim majority areas, even when compared to nearby villages with a Hindu majority. Muslims on average received only two-thirds the loan amounts disbursed to other minorities. The proportion of Muslims living in pucca houses is lower than the general population, both in cities and in villages, even if compared to others at their level of poverty. Muslims form less than 3% of IAS officers and 4% of IPS officers, even though their population is about 13% of the total.

Overall, the Sachar Committee concluded that on average Muslims are at roughly the same socio-economic level as Dalits and adivasis.

Similarly, in a study published in the *Economic and Political Weekly* in 2007, the authors responded to 548 job advertisements from private sector companies with three identical applications—one with a high caste Hindu name, one with a Dalit name, and one with a Muslim name. Even though the applications were otherwise identical, the Dalit name was approximately one-third less likely to get called for an interview, and the Muslim name was two-thirds less likely.

In both the public and the private sectors, Muslims are denied opportunities across the board. There is no evidence of "appeasement", only evidence of discrimination.

**Myth:** "But Hindus cannot buy land in Jammu and Kashmir!"

**Non-Kashmiris** cannot buy land in J&K—just as non-Himachalis cannot buy land in Himachal Pradesh, outsiders cannot even enter Nagaland or Mizoram without permission, non-Uttarakhandis can buy only small plots in Uttarakhand, etc. Many parts of India have these regulations to protect local populations. The issue has nothing to do with religion.

**Myth:** "The Muslim population is increasing faster than the Hindu population, especially because Muslim men can have many wives. Their aim is to become the majority."

The National Family Health Survey has found that young Muslim women have the same fertility rate as young Hindu women of the same economic level. The slightly higher growth rate for Muslims overall is due to the fact that, on average, Muslims are poorer than Hindus. Common sense would also indicate this. Kerala, which has a Muslim population of approximately 25%, also has the lowest population growth rate of any state in the country.

Poverty and lack of facilities are far more important than religion in deciding how many children you have. The fertility rate of Muslims in states like Tamil Nadu and Kerala is far below that of Hindus in Uttar Pradesh, Bihar or Rajasthan, for instance.

As for Muslim men marrying many wives, it is blindingly obvious that this can make no difference to population growth—if one Muslim man has two wives, that means some other man will have no wife (given that the populations of men and women in each community are roughly equal). Meanwhile, the NFHS found (in the only survey that looked at this) that approximately 5.8% of Hindu men have multiple wives, while only 5.73% of Muslim men do.

**Myth:** "Muslims got 'their' country when Pakistan was created, now they should leave 'our' country."

The first active political leaders to talk of separate countries for Muslims and Hindus were those who would later be part of the Hindu Mahasabha. Bhai Paramanand, later president of the Mahasabha, demanded this in 1905. At that time, there was no Muslim League and Mohammad Ali Jinnah was part of the Congress. Jinnah and the Muslim League did not change their minds until 1940, thirty-five years later. Even then, huge numbers of Muslims opposed the idea of Pakistan, including the biggest Islamic religious school in India—the Deoband seminary—and President of the Congress Party, Maulana Azad, who was one of India's greatest freedom fighters. The demand for Pakistan was a demand by a political party, not a demand by Muslims as a whole.

# Bibliography

Ambedkar, B.R. (2004). *The Annihilation of Caste.* New York: Columbia University Centre for New Media Teaching and Learning. Available online at http://ccnmtl.columbia.edu/projects/mmt/ambedkar/web/readings/aoc_print_2004.pdf, last accessed on November 7, 2016.

Basu, Amrita (1998). "Hindu Women's Activism in India and the Questions It Raises", in ed. Sarkar, Tanika and Basu, Amrita. *Resisting the Sacred and the Secular: Women's Activism and Politicised Religion in South Asia.* New Delhi: Kali for Women.

Basu, Tapan, Datta, Pradip, Sarkar, Sumit, Sarkar, Tanika and Sen, Sambuddha (1993). *Khaki Shorts, Saffron Flags.* New Delhi: Orient Longman, Tracts for the Times Series.

Casolari, Marzia (2000). "Hindutva's Foreign Tie-Up in the 1930s: Archival Evidence", *Economic and Political Weekly.* Mumbai: Sameeksha Trust. January 22.

Chandrasekhar, C.P. and Ghosh, Jayati (2000). *The Market That Failed: Neoliberal Economic Reforms in India.* New Delhi: Leftword.

Davis, Richard (2005). "The Cultural Background of Hindutva", in ed. Oldenburg, Philip K. and Ayres, Alyssa, *India Briefing: Takeoff At Last?* M.E. Sharpe.

ENS (2016). "Wait Continues: Private Sector Investment Slows", *Indian Express.* July 5.

Golwalkar, M.S. ('Guruji') (1979). "Integral Man", in Upadhyaya, D., Golwalkar, M.S., Thengadi, D.B. *The Integral Approach.* New Delhi: Deendayal Research Institute.

Golwalkar, M.S. (n.d.). *Bunch of Thoughts,* Third Edition. Nagpur: Rashtriya Swayamsevak Sangh. Available online at http://www.rss.org, last accessed on November 7, 2016.

Gopalakrishnan, Shankar (2008). *Hindutva and Neoliberalism: Fascism, Free Markets and the Restructuring of Indian Capitalism.* Aakar Books.

Gopalakrishnan, Shankar (2013). "Why Do They Love Narendra Modi?", *Kafila*. August 24. Available online at https://kafila.online/2013/08/24/why-do-they-love-narendra-modi-shankar-gopalakrishnan/.

Gopalakrishnan, Shankar (2015). "The Growing Threats to India's Financial System From Easy Access to Land and Natural Resources", Rights and Resources Initiative. Available online at http://rightsandresources.org/en/publication/view/the-growing-threats-to-indias-financial-system-easy-access-and-clearances-of-land-and-natural-resources-2/.

Gopalakrishnan, Shankar (2016b). 'The Politics of Fear and Hate Hidden in Demonetisation", *The Wire*. December 6. Available online at: https://thewire.in/84712/the-politics-of-fear-and-hate-hidden-in-demonetisation/

Gopalakrishnan,Shankar (2016a). "Demonetisation is a permanent transfer of wealth from the poor to the rich", *Scroll.in*. November 25. Available online at: https://scroll.in/article/822402/demonetisation-is-a-permanent-transfer-of-wealth-from-the-poor-to-the-rich

Gramsci, Antonio, tr. Hoare, Quentin and Smith, Geoffrey Nowell (1971). *Selections from the Prison Notebooks*. London: Lawrence & Wishart.

Heath, Oliver; Kumar, Sanjay; and Yadav, Yogendra (1999). "The BJP's New Social Bloc", *Frontline*. Chennai: Kasturi and Sons, November 6–19.

Jaffrelot, Christophe (1998). *The Hindu Nationalist Movement in India*. New York: Columbia University Press.

Jain, Mayank (2016). "Indian Industry is on Life Support—and the Government's Denial of This isn't Helping", *Scroll.in*. October 13.

Janardhanan, Arun (2017). "Demonetisation: 35 per cent job losses, 50 per cent revenue dip, says study by largest organisation of manufacturers", *Indian Express*, January 9.

Jenkins, Rob (1999). *Democratic Politics and Economic Reform in India*. Cambridge: Cambridge University Press.

Jessop, Bob (1982). *The Capitalist State*: *Marxist Theories and Methods*. Oxford: Blackwell.

Jha, Dhirendra K. (2016). "In Wake of Attacks, RSS Shakhas See Sudden Disappearance of Dalits", *Scroll.in*. September 6. Available online at http://scroll.in/article/815767/in-wake-of-attacks-rss-shakhas-see-sudden-disappearance-of-dalits, last accessed on November 9, 2016.

Masood, Bashaarat (2016). "Kashmir Witnesses Biggest Crackdown in Two Decades, More Than 446 Arrested in a Week", *Indian Express*. October 21.

Mussolini, Benito (1932). *The Doctrine of Fascism*. Encyclopedia Italiana. English translation available online at http://www.indiana.edu/~hist104/sources/Mussolini.html.

Nadkarni, M.V. (1987). *Farmers' Movements in India*. Ahmedabad: Allied Publishers Pvt. Ltd.

Palshikar, Suhas (2004). "Majoritarian Middle Ground?", *Economic and Political Weekly*. Mumbai: Sameeksha Trust. December 18.

Poulantzas, Nicos (1978). tr. Camiller, Patrick. *State, Power, Socialism*. Paris: Presses Universitaires de France. Reprinted by Verso in 2000.

Rajagopal, Arvind (1999). "Brand Logics and the Cultural Forms of Political Society in India", *Social Text*. Durham: Duke University Press, 17:3.

Roychowdhury, Anamitra (2014). "A Reality Check on the Labour Market Flexibility Argument in India", *Vikalp–People's Perspectives for Change*. January.

*Scroll.in* (2015). "No Acche Din for Rural India Under the Modi Government, Data Indicates", *Scroll.in*. January 8.

Shah, Rajiv (2007). "'Karmayogi' Swears by Caste Order", *Times of India*, November 24.

Sharma, Supriya (2014). "Hiring and Firing Workers was Never Difficult in Rajasthan, Data Shows", *Scroll.in*. August 24.

Singh, Siddhartha and Pradhan, Bibhudatta (2017). "India Said to Get 97% Banned Notes in Setback to Graft Crackdown", *Bloomberg News*. January 4.

Swamy, Subramaniam (2000). "Unlearnt Lessons of the Emergency", *The Hindu*. June 13.

*The Economist* (2016). "Dry Times", *The Economist*. April 30th.

Thengadi, D.B. (1979). "Integral Humanism – A Study" in Upadhyaya, D., Golwalkar, M.S., Thengadi, D.B. *The Integral Approach*. New Delhi: Deendayal Research Institute.

Upadhyaya, Deendayal (1979). "Integral Humanism", in Upadhyaya, D., Golwalkar, M.S., Thengadi, D.B. *The Integral Approach*. New Delhi: Deendayal Research Institute.

Upadhyaya, Deendayal (1979b). "Harmony Between the Individual and the Collectivity", in Upadhyaya, D., Golwalkar, M.S., Thengadi, D.B. *The Integral Approach*. New Delhi: Deendayal Research Institute.

Yadav, Yogendra (2004). "The Elusive Mandate of 2004", *Economic and Political Weekly*. Mumbai: Sameeksha Trust. December 18.